09-018

Senior Author
Jennette MacKenzie

Senior Consultant
Miriam P. Trehearne

Senior Consultant
Carmel Crévola

Series Consultants
Ruth McQuirter Scott—*Word Study*
James Coulter—*Assessment*
Neil Andersen—*Media*
Maureen Innes—*ESL/ELL*
Rod Peturson—*Science*
Nancy Christoffer—*Bias and Equity*

Series Writing Team
Paula S. Goepfert, *Senior Writer*
Kathleen Corrigan
James Coulter
Dianne Dillabough
Lalie Harcourt
Jane Hutchison
Christel Kleitsch
Wendy Mathieu
Christine McClymont
Sarah Peterson
Liz Powell
Ricki Wortzman

Australia   Canada   Mexico   Singapore   Spain   United Kingdom   United States

Nelson Literacy 4b

Jennette MacKenzie

Director of Publishing
Beverley Buxton

General Manager, Literacy and Reference
Kevin Martindale

Director of Publishing, Literacy and Reference
Joe Banel

Publisher, Literacy
Rivka Cranley

Executive Managing Editor, Development
Darleen Rotozinski

Senior Product Manager
Mark Cressman

Senior Program Manager
Norma Kennedy

Developmental Editors
Laura Edlund
David MacDonald
Kim Toffan

Researchers
Monika Croydon
Susan Hughes
Monica Kulling
Catherine Rondina

Editorial Assistants
Petal Almeida
Corry Codner
Lisa Peterson
Rebecca Roberts

Executive Director, Content and Media Production
Renate McCloy

Director, Content and Media Production
Lisa Dimson

Senior Content Production Manager
Carol Martin

Proofreader
Elizabeth d'Anjou

Production Manager
Cathy Deak

Director, Asset Management Services
Vicki Gould

Design Director
Ken Phipps

Managing Designer
Sasha Moroz

Series Design
Sasha Moroz
Steven Savicky

Series Wordmark
Steven Savicky

Cover Design
Sasha Moroz

Interior Design
Andrew Adams
Brian Cartwright
Claudia Dávila
Susan Hedley
Courtney Hellam
Richard Hockney
Eugene Lo
Sasha Moroz
Roberto Pagliero
Peter Papayanakis
Peggy Rhodes
Jan John Rivera
Steven Savicky
Glenn Toddun
Art Plus Ltd.
Studio Montage

Art Buyer
Suzanne Peden

Production Specialist
Maria Castelli

Compositor
Courtney Hellam

Photo Research and Permissions
Karen Becker
Patricia Buckley

Printer
Transcontinental Printing

COPYRIGHT © 2007 by Nelson, a division of Thomson Canada Limited.

ISBN-13: 978-0-17-629101-3
ISBN-10: 0-17-629101-6

Printed and bound in Canada
3   4   10 09 08 07

For more information contact Thomson Nelson, 1120 Birchmount Road, Toronto, Ontario, M1K 5G4. Or you can visit our Internet site at http://www.nelson.com

ALL RIGHTS RESERVED. No part of this work covered by the copyright herein, except for any reproducible pages included in this work, may be reproduced, transcribed, or used in any form or by any means—graphic, electronic, or mechanical, including photocopying, recording, taping, Web distribution, or information storage and retrieval systems—without the written permission of the publisher.

For permission to use material from this text or product, submit a request online at www.thomsonrights.com

Every effort has been made to trace ownership of all copyrighted material and to secure permission from copyright holders. In the event of any question arising as to the use of any material, we will be pleased to make the necessary corrections in future printings.

Advisers and Reviewers: Ontario

Wendy Bedford, Peterborough Victoria Northumberland and Clarington CDSB, ON

Debra Boddy, Toronto DSB, ON

Maggie Boss, Dufferin-Peel CDSB, ON

Karen Byromshaw, Toronto DSB, ON

Mary Cairo, Toronto CDSB, ON

Genevieve Dowson, Hamilton-Wentworth CDSB, ON

Denise Edwards, Toronto DSB, ON

Lorraine Giroux, District School Board of Niagara, ON

Charmaine Graves, Thames Valley DSB, ON

Colleen Hayward, Toronto CDSB, ON

Charmaine Hung, Toronto DSB, ON

Eddie Ing, Toronto DSB, ON

Sue Jackson, Thames Valley DSB, ON

Lee Jones-Imhotep, Toronto DSB, ON

Tania Korostil, Peel DSB, ON

Luci Lackey, Upper Grand DSB, ON

Laurie Light, Dufferin-Peel CDSB, ON

Lorrie Lowes, Ottawa-Carleton DSB, ON

Maria Makuch, Ottawa-Carleton DSB, ON

Jennifer Mandarino, Dufferin-Peel CDSB, ON

Carolyn March, Hamilton-Wentworth DSB, ON

Mary Marshall, Halton DSB, ON

Thérèse McNamara, Simcoe County DSB, ON

Andrew Mildenberger, Toronto DSB, ON

Laura Mossey, Durham DSB, ON

Elisena Mycroft, Hamilton-Wentworth DSB, ON

Mary Anne Olah, Toronto DSB, ON

Judy Onody, Toronto CDSB, ON

Eleanor Pardoe, Grand Erie DSB, ON

Krista Pedersen, Upper Canada DSB, ON

Catherine Pollock, Toronto DSB, ON

Cheryl Potvin, Ottawa-Carleton DSB, ON

Tara Rajaram-Donaldson, Toronto DSB, ON

Joanne Saragosa, Toronto CDSB, ON

Katherine Shaw, Peel DSB, ON

Jackie Stafford, Toronto DSB, ON

Sandra VandeCamp, Dufferin-Peel CDSB, ON

Ann Varty, Trillium Lakelands DSB, ON

Contents

6 Welcome to *Nelson Literacy*

LITERATURE

7 Legends

8 **Create a Legend**
Graphic Story

10 **The Story of William Tell**
Legend retold by James Baldwin

13 **China's Bravest Girl: The Legend of Hua Mu Lan**
Legend retold by Charlie Chin

18 **Writing with a Strong Voice**
Writing Strategy

20 **The Swords of King Arthur**
*Graphic Legend
retold by Barbara Spurll*

23 **Legends Live On**
Media Focus

25 **The Minotaur**
*Legend
retold by Anne Rockwell*

28 **The Little Hero of Holland**
*Legend
adapted from a story
by Etta Austin Blaisdell and
Mary Frances Blaisdell*

34 **Making Inferences While You Listen**
Listening Strategy

35 **The Woman Who Outshone the Sun**
*Legend retold by
Alejandro Cruz Martinez*

SCIENCE

41 Light

42 **Open Your Eyes to Light!**
Illustration

44 **Where Does Light Come From?**
Informational Report

46 **What Does Light Travel Through?**
*Procedural Text
by Sally Nankivell-Aston
and Dorothy Jackson*

49 **Asking Questions**
*Speaking and Listening
Strategy*

50 **Using Formal or Informal Voice**
Writing Strategy

52 **Facts of Light**
*Informational Report
by Lorraine Cameron*

55 **Mr. Microscope's Reflections on Bike Safety**
Interview by Annie Chan

58 **The Colours of Light**
Informational Report

60 **Rainbow Riddle**
Short Story by Sheilah Currie

62 **The Wonder of Fireflies**
Media Focus

64 **Tips for Making a Video**
*Informational Report by Mark
Shulman and Hazlitt Krog*

SOCIAL STUDIES

67 Canada's Regions

68 "Eh" Is for Canada
Photo Collage

70 A Map of Canada's Regions and Resources
Map

72 The Canadian Shield
Informational Report
by Susan Hughes

75 The Interior Plains
Informational Report
by Susan Hughes

77 Using Sensory Words
Writing Strategy

78 The Seas We Share
Poem by Robert Heidbreder

80 Fox on the Ice
Adventure Story
by Tomson Highway

84 Guy's Ontario Adventure
Travel Journal
by Vivien Bowers

90 Powwow!
Factual Recount/Photo Essay
by Laura Edlund and Nance Ackerman

94 Send a Postcard!
Media Focus

96 By Truck to the North
Factual Recount
by Andy Turnbull with Debora Pearson

SCIENCE

101 Sound

102 Sound Check
Illustration

104 A World Full of Sound
Informational Report
by David Louis Dreier

107 Bouncing Back
Informational Explanation
by Barbara Taylor

109 Choosing Strong Verbs
Writing Strategy

110 Sound the Alarm!
Informational Report

112 Noise Day
Poem
by Shel Silverstein

114 FAQ: Sound
Informational Explanation
by Etta Kaner

117 School of Sound
Interview
by Laura Edlund

120 Sounding Off
Media Focus

122 Making Meaning Clear
Speaking Strategy

123 Musical Sounds
Procedural Text
by Julian Rowe and Molly Perham

127 Credits

94

123

Welcome to Nelson Literacy

Your *Nelson Literacy* book is full of fascinating stories and articles. Many of the topics are the same as those you will study in science and social studies.

Here are the different kinds of pages you will see in this book:

Let's Talk
Here's a chance to have some fun and also show what you know.

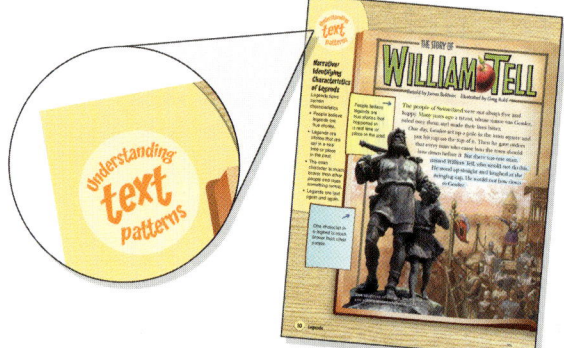

Understanding Strategies
These pages introduce you to reading, writing, speaking, listening, and media literacy strategies. Some pages have sticky notes with hints about the strategies.

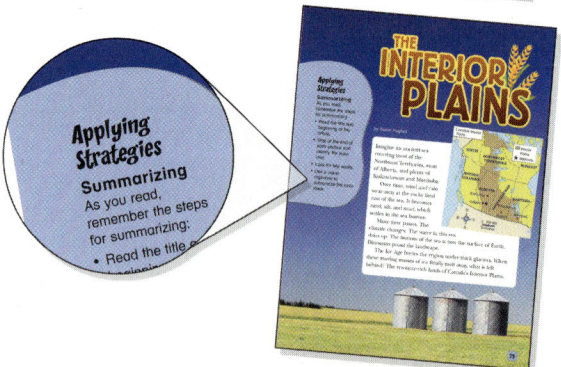

Applying Strategies
These pages give you the chance to try out the strategies you've learned.

Putting It All Together
At the end of each unit, you'll have the chance to use the strategies that you've learned.

Legends

Literature

In this unit, you will

- identify characteristics of legends
- write with a strong voice
- explain why different audiences respond differently to media texts
- make inferences while you read
- make inferences while you listen

However, the hero Kroo led a revolt and got rid of the king.

However, the hero Taja made the king see the error of his ways.

However, the hero Taja killed the beast with one deadly arrow.

However, the hero Kroo caught the band and made them return the loot and help the poor.

However, the hero Kroo's experiments uncovered a cure.

However, the hero Taja found the cause of the sickness.

And so the legend of Kroo was retold for centuries.

And so the legend of Taja was retold for centuries.

Understanding text patterns

Narrative: Identifying Characteristics of Legends

Legends have certain characteristics:

- People believe legends are true stories.
- Legends are stories that are set in a real time or place in the past.
- The main character is much braver than other people and does something heroic.
- Legends are told again and again.

THE STORY OF WILLIAM TELL

Retold by James Baldwin   Illustrated by Greg Ruhl

> People believe legends are true stories that happened in a real time or place in the past.

The people of Switzerland were not always free and happy. Many years ago a tyrant, whose name was Gessler, ruled over them and made their lives bitter.

One day, Gessler set up a pole in the town square and put his cap on the top of it. Then he gave orders that every man who came into the town should bow down before it. But there was one man, named William Tell, who would not do this. He stood up straight and laughed at the swinging cap. He would not bow down to Gessler.

> One character in a legend is much braver than other people.

This sculpture of William Tell and his son stands in Altdorf, Switzerland.

10 Legends

When Gessler heard this, he was very angry. He was afraid that other people would disobey, and that soon the whole country would rise up against him. So he made up his mind to punish the bold William Tell.

Now, William Tell was a famous hunter. No one in all the land could shoot with a crossbow and arrow as well as he. Gessler knew this, and so he thought of a cruel plan. He ordered that Tell's young son should be made to stand up in the town square with an apple on his head. Gessler told Tell to shoot the apple with one of his arrows.

Tell begged Gessler not to test him in this way. What if the boy moved? What if Tell's hand trembled? What if the arrow did not fly straight? "Will you make me kill my boy?" Tell asked.

"Say no more," said Gessler. "You must hit the apple with one arrow. If you fail, my soldiers shall kill the boy before your eyes."

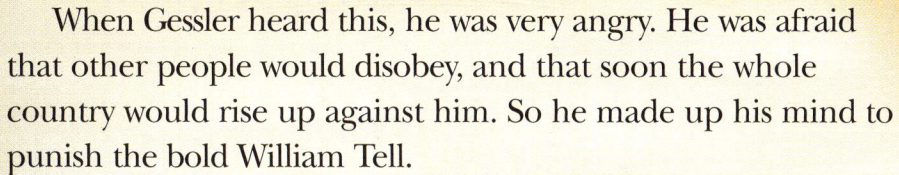
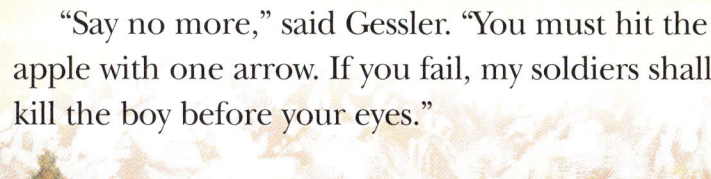

The main character does something heroic.

The brave acts of legendary characters are told again and again. Often, there is more than one story about a legendary character.

Tell fitted the arrow to his crossbow. He took aim and let it fly. The boy stood firm and still. He was not afraid because he had complete faith in his father's skill.

The arrow whistled through the air. It struck the apple in the centre and carried it away. The people who saw it shouted with joy.

As Tell turned to leave the square, an arrow that he had hidden under his coat dropped to the ground.

"Fellow!" cried Gessler. "What do you mean to do with this second arrow?"

"Tyrant!" was Tell's proud answer. "This arrow was for your heart if I had hurt my child!"

And there is an old story that, not long after this, Tell did shoot Gessler with one of his arrows, and so set his country free.

CHINA'S BRAVEST GIRL: THE LEGEND OF HUA MU LAN

Retold by Charlie Chin
Illustrated by Tomie Arai

Applying Strategies

Narrative: Identifying Characteristics of Legends

As you read, look for these characteristics of legends:

- People believe legends are true stories.
- Legends are stories that are set in a real time or place in the past.
- The main character is much braver than other people and does something heroic.
- Legends are told again and again.

The sound is click, and again, click click,
young Hua Mu Lan at the loom.
Her fingers fly, the shuttle darts,
as she weaves inside her room.

Last night she saw the notice.
It was posted on the wall.
On it was her father's name.
He must answer the emperor's call.

The enemy has invaded China.
Our army must prepare to fight.
One man from every household
must be ready by morning light.

Her father is old and tired.
His hair is turning white.
She tells him of her plan
as they talk by candlelight.

"I am young and healthy,
and you have no eldest son.
If the emperor needs a soldier,
then I must be the one."

For love of her elderly father
she will dress in warrior's clothes,
walking and talking like a man,
so no one ever knows.

The bravest girl in China
puts away the perfumed comb.
To repay her father's kindness
she will ride away from home.

She joins ten thousand soldiers
camped in the moonlit snow.
Their tents shine like lanterns
lit by the campfire glow.

The morning light brings the battle.
The invaders take the field.
Enemy arrows find their mark.
China's line begins to yield.

When all seems lost a shout is heard.
"Brave sons of China follow me!"
Warriors wheel and turn about
like the waves of an angry sea.

Cheering troops rally around her.
The enemy line breaks in fear.
Hua Mu Lan's courage wins the day
as she fights with her sword and spear.

She wins in a hundred battles.
Ten years like arrows fly by.
She gains the rank of general.
Her legend will never die.

The emperor summons his "hero"
to receive from the royal hand
a minister's post and the title
to a nobleman's house and land.

"There is nothing that I desire,
neither wealth nor minister's post.
My duty is to my father.
In old age, he needs me most."

The news is heard at her father's gate
where colourful lanterns burn.
Her family prepares a feast
to celebrate her return.

She enters as a general.
Her father watches with pride.
She greets her father and mother,
then turns to go inside.

Alone in her room at last,
she sits on her childhood bed.
She takes off the iron helmet
and places flowers on her head.

The ocean hides the oyster.
The oyster hides a pearl.
Bright armour and heavy helmet
hid China's bravest girl.

Reflect on

Strategies: How did thinking about legends help you understand this story? Find three places in the story that match the characteristics of a legend.

Connections: Why do you think people make movies and video games about legendary heroes?

Writing with a Strong Voice

When you listen, you notice things right away about a person's voice. Someone may sound serious or goofy or enthusiastic, for example. Writing has voice, too. A strong voice gives writing energy and personality.

Here are three short pieces of writing about Robin Hood, the famous robber who lived in Sherwood Forest. Each piece of writing has a strong voice.

When you finish reading, look back. Notice how a sentence from one piece wouldn't "fit" in another piece. That's because each one has a strong voice.

> This author's voice is factual and serious. What might that tell you about this author's purpose?

Robin Hood was a legendary English outlaw who stole from the rich and gave to the poor. He is the subject of countless ballads and stories, some dating as far back as the 1300s.

From *The World Book Encyclopedia*

> This author's voice is descriptive. She uses words like "knave" and "merry men" to create a feeling that the story happened long ago. What might that tell you about this author's purpose?

One day, long ago, the king of England summoned the sheriff of Nottingham to his court.

"I hear a bold outlaw named Robin Hood hides in Sherwood Forest," the king said. "The knave and his band of merry men make a sport of robbing my wealthy subjects, and then giving their loot to the poor. What have you done about him?"

From *Robin Hood and His Merry Men* by Mary Pope Osborne

Long long ago, in Sherwood Forest in the county of Nottinghamshire, there lived a man who was known as Robin Hood, probably because he liked robin people. He had a wife called Maid Marian, probably because Robin made her keen on marian him.

From *Robin Hood and His Miserable Men* by Dick King-Smith

This author's voice is joking. He plays with words like "robin" and "marian," and he doesn't take the great Robin Hood too seriously. What might that tell you about this author's purpose?

How to write with a strong voice:

- ☑ Think about your purpose. Do you want to inform or entertain your readers?
- ☑ Choose words that match your purpose.
- ☑ Write your sentences in a way that shows your attitude to the subject. Do you feel respectful or playful?
- ☑ Listen to your own writing. Does every sentence match the voice you have chosen?

Reflect on

Writer's Craft: Describe the author's voice. Give examples from the graphic story to support your ideas.

Critical Literacy: How would your reaction to the legend change if the characters' words were left out?

Understanding media

Explaining Why Different Audiences Respond Differently to Media Texts

Legends Live On

Legends live on in movies and video games. But not everyone enjoys the same movie or game. You may think a movie is funny, while your older brother thinks it's silly. You may think a video game is perfect for you, but your parents say the rating on the box means you can't play it.

Different audiences react in different ways to the same movie or video game. Think about how different audiences might react to this advertisement for the movie *King Arthur*.

Making connections helps people decide if they want to see a movie. What connections do you think a boy would make to this advertisement? What connections do you think a girl would make?

Making inferences helps people decide if a movie is appropriate for a certain audience. What inferences do you think parents might make about this movie?

Ratings, such as G and PG, give an idea about the age of the audience the movie was made for. Do you think you and your parents would give this movie the same rating?

Think about *your* reaction to this video-game box. Now think about other people you know. How do you think *they* might react to this game box?

Understanding reading strategies

Making Inferences

Making inferences is sometimes called "reading between the lines." An author may not tell you everything. You can use clues from the text and your own knowledge to make inferences and draw your own conclusions.

> Clues from the text and your own knowledge help you draw conclusions. How do you think the king and queen felt about the Minotaur?

THE MINOTAUR

Retold by Anne Rockwell   Illustrated by Paul McCusker

Long ago, on the island of Crete, a queen gave birth to a child with the body of a baby boy and the head of a bull calf.

The baby grew up to be a monster who lived on nothing but human flesh. He was called the Minotaur.

This royal monster was so dangerous that the king and queen hired an architect named Daedalus to build a twisting maze within the palace walls. The Minotaur's room was deep in the maze so that he could never escape, but neither could his victims.

Across the sea was the city of Athens. The people of Athens and Crete were enemies. To keep the peace, the king and queen of Crete demanded that every year seven boys and seven girls from Athens be sent across the sea to be fed to the Minotaur.

> Clues from the text and your own knowledge help you draw conclusions. Why would the people of Athens send their young to Crete?

A character's actions can tell you about that character's personality. What do Theseus's actions tell you about him? →

One year, a young prince named Theseus was among the Athenians picked to be sacrificed. But Theseus was not planning to die. Instead, he plotted to kill the Minotaur.

The king and queen of Crete had a daughter, Princess Ariadne, who fell in love with the handsome victim. She secretly offered to help Theseus kill the monster, on condition that Theseus marry her. He agreed, so Ariadne gave him a ball of fine silk thread and a sharp sword and told him what to do.

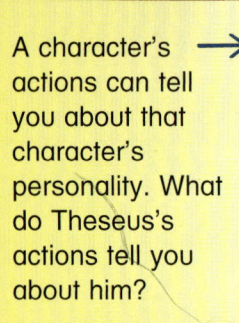

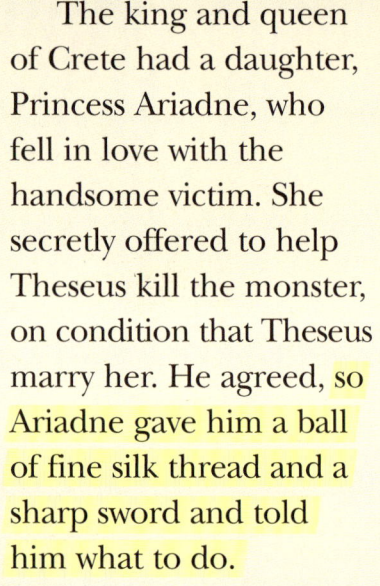

↑
Your personal experiences can help you understand a character. Have you ever known a "take charge" kind of person like Ariadne?

As he entered the maze, Theseus trailed the thread behind him until he reached the place where the monster lay sleeping.

He grabbed the Minotaur by the hair and killed him. Then Theseus escaped by following the thread, which led him out again.

He and his companions boarded their ship, and Ariadne went with them. Theseus returned home, a great hero.

The Little Hero of Holland

Adapted from a story by Etta Austin Blaisdell and Mary Frances Blaisdell
Illustrated by Katherine Brown

Applying Strategies

Making Inferences

As you read this legend, make inferences to help you understand what you are reading:

- Use clues from the text.
- Use your own personal knowledge.
- Use the character's actions to infer about the character's personality.

Holland is a country where much of the land lies below sea level. Only great walls called dikes keep the North Sea from rushing in and flooding the land. For centuries, the people of Holland have worked to keep the walls strong. Even the little children know the dikes must be watched every moment, and that a hole no larger than your finger can be a very dangerous thing.

Many years ago, there lived in Holland a boy named Peter. Peter's father was one of the men who tended the gates in the dikes, called sluices. He opened and closed the sluices.

One afternoon in the early fall, when Peter was 8 years old, his mother called him from his play. "Come, Peter," she said. "I want you to take these cakes to your friend, the blind man. If you go quickly, and do not stop to play, you will be home again before dark."

The boy was glad to go on such an errand, and started off with a light heart. He stayed with his friend a little while to tell him about his walk along the dike and about the sun and the flowers and the ships far out at sea. Then he remembered his mother's words. Saying goodbye to his friend, Peter set out for home.

As Peter walked beside the canal, he noticed how the rains had raised the waters in the canal. He saw how the waters beat against the side of the dike, and he thought of his father's gates.

"I am glad they are so strong," he said to himself. "If they gave way, what would become of us? These fields would be covered with water. Father always calls the waters the 'angry waters.' I suppose he thinks they are angry at him for keeping them out so long."

As he walked along, he sometimes stopped to pick the blue flowers that grew beside the canal, or to listen to the rabbits' soft tread as they rustled through the grass. But more often he smiled as he thought of his visit to his friend.

Suddenly he noticed that the sun was setting, and that it was growing dark. He began to run toward home.

Just then he heard a noise. He stopped and looked down. He could see a small hole in the dike and water trickling through it.

Any child in Holland is frightened at the thought of a leak in the dike.

Peter understood the danger at once. If the water ran through a little hole it would soon make a larger one, and the whole country would be flooded. In a moment he saw what he must do. Throwing away his flowers, he climbed down the side of the dike and thrust his finger into the tiny hole.

The stream of water stopped!

"Oho!" he said to himself. "The angry waters must stay back now. I can keep them back with my finger. Holland shall not be drowned while I am here."

This was all very well at first, but it soon grew dark and cold. Young Peter shouted and screamed. "Come here! Come here," he called. But no one heard him; no one came to help him.

It grew still colder, and his arm ached and began to grow stiff and numb. He shouted again, "Will no one come? Mother! Mother!"

Peter's mother had looked anxiously for him along the dike road many times since sunset. But she decided that he must be spending the night at his friend's. She closed and locked the cottage door, and planned to scold Peter in the morning for staying away from home without her permission.

Peter tried to whistle, but his teeth chattered. He thought of his brother and sister in their warm beds, and of his dear father and mother. "I must not let them be drowned," he thought. "I must stay here until someone comes, even if I have to stay all night."

The moon and stars looked down on the child crouching on a stone on the side of the dike. His head was bent, and his eyes were closed, but he was not asleep, for every now and then he rubbed the hand that was holding back the angry sea.

"I'll stand it somehow," he thought. So he stayed there all night keeping the water out.

Early the next morning, a man going to work thought he heard a groan as he walked along the top of the dike. Looking over the edge, he saw a child clinging to the side of the great wall.

"What's the matter?" he called. "Are you hurt?"

"There's a leak in the dike. I'm keeping the water back!" Peter yelled. "Please get help quickly!"

The news spread. People came running with shovels, and the hole was soon mended.

Peter was carried home to his parents, and before long, the whole town knew how he had saved their lives that night. To this day, they have never forgotten the brave little hero of Holland.

A statue of the little hero of Holland stands in the city of Spaarndam.

Reflect on

Strategies: What did you learn about Peter by "reading between the lines"? Find the words or sentences that helped you make these inferences.

Your Learning: What have you learned about Holland by reading this story?

Making Inferences While You Listen

Making inferences while you listen helps you understand what you hear.

Sometimes the speaker does not tell you everything. When you listen, you use clues from what the speaker is saying and how the speaker is saying it, plus your own knowledge, to "listen between the lines."

> LONG AGO, IN 1950, MY GREAT-AUNT VIOLET LIVED ON THE RED RIVER IN MANITOBA. SHE WAS TINY, BUT HAD MUSCLES OF STEEL AND A WILL TO MATCH.

GILLIAN IS TALKING FAST. SHE'S EXCITED TO TELL US HER STORY.

> THE RED RIVER OFTEN FLOODS, BUT THAT YEAR GREAT-AUNT VIOLET FEARED A DISASTER. IN FACT, THE RED RIVER IS USUALLY ABOUT 150 METRES WIDE. DURING THE FLOOD, IT WAS 65 KILOMETRES WIDE!

GILLIAN KNOWS A LOT ABOUT THIS EVENT.

HER FAMILY PROBABLY TALKS ABOUT THIS OFTEN.

> GREAT-AUNT VIOLET PUT ON A RAINCOAT AND SAT IN THE OLD ROWBOAT THAT WAS IN THE BACKYARD. WHEN THE WATERS WERE HIGH ENOUGH TO FLOAT THE BOAT, SHE STARTED ROWING.

HER GREAT-AUNT REMINDS ME OF MY GRANDMA. THEY'RE BOTH DETERMINED.

> GREAT-AUNT VIOLET ROWED FOR 20 HOURS. SHE RESCUED 14 CHILDREN FROM FLOODED HOMES. SHE BECAME A LEGEND IN HER OWN TIME!

GILLIAN IS REALLY PROUD OF HER GREAT-AUNT.

How to make inferences while you listen:

- ☑ Listen to the tone and speed of the speaker's voice.
- ☑ Watch the speaker's face and gestures.
- ☑ Listen for words that give you clues to the speaker's feelings and point of view.
- ☑ Connect to what you already know.

The Woman Who Outshone the Sun

The Legend of Lucia Zenteno

Retold by Alejandro Cruz Martinez
Translated by Rosalma Zubizarreta
Illustrated by Fernando Olivera

Putting It All Together

As you read this story, remember the strategies you've learned in this unit:
- Think about the characteristics of legends.
- Make inferences.
- Identify the voice of the story.

The day Lucia Zenteno arrived, everyone in the village was astonished. No one knew where she came from. Yet they all saw that she was amazingly beautiful, and that she brought thousands of dancing butterflies and brightly coloured flowers on her skirts. She walked softly yet with quiet dignity, her long, unbraided hair flowing behind her. A loyal iguana walked at her side.

No one knew who she was, but they did know that nothing shone as brightly as Lucia Zenteno. Some people said that Lucia Zenteno outshone the sun. Others said that her glorious hair seemed to block out the light.

Everyone felt a little afraid of someone so wonderful and yet so strange.

There used to be a river that ran by the town, almost the same river that runs by there now. And people said that when Lucia Zenteno went there to bathe, the river fell in love with her. The water rose from its bed and began to flow through her shining black hair.

When Lucia finished bathing, she would sit by the river and comb out her hair with a comb made from the wood of the mesquite tree. And when she did, the water, the fishes, and the otters would flow out of her hair and return to the river once more.

The old people of the village said that, although Lucia was different from them, she should be honoured and treated with respect. She understood the ways of nature, they said.

But some people did not listen to the Elders. They were afraid of Lucia's powers, which they did not understand. And so they refused to answer Lucia's greetings, or offer their friendship. They called her cruel names and spied on her day and night.

Lucia did not return the meanness of the people. She kept to herself and continued to walk with her head held high.

Her quiet dignity angered some of the people. They whispered that Lucia must be trying to harm them. People became more afraid of Lucia and so they treated her more cruelly. Finally, they drove her from the village.

Lucia went down to the river one last time to say goodbye. As always, the water rose to greet her and began to flow through her glorious hair. But this time, when she tried to comb the river out of her hair, the river would not leave her.

And so, when Lucia Zenteno left the village, the river and the fishes and the otters went with her, leaving only a dry, winding riverbed, a serpent of sand where the water had been.

Everyone saw that Lucia Zenteno was leaving and that the river, the fishes, and the otters were leaving with her. The people were filled with despair. They had never imagined that their beautiful river would ever leave them, no matter what they did.

Where once there had been green trees and cool breezes, now no more rain fell, no birds sang, no otters played. The people and their animals suffered from thirst. People began to understand, as never before, how much the river, the fishes, the otters, even the trees and birds had meant to the village. They began to understand how much the river had loved Lucia Zenteno.

The Elders said that everyone must search for Lucia and beg her forgiveness. Some people did not want to. They were too afraid. But when the drought continued, everyone finally agreed to follow the Elders' advice. And so the whole village set out in search of Lucia.

After many days of walking, the people found the iguana cave where Lucia had gone to seek refuge. Lucia was waiting for them, but they could not see her face. She had turned her back to the people.

At first no one dared to say a word. Then two children called out, "Lucia, we have come to ask your forgiveness. Please have mercy on us and return our river!"

Lucia Zenteno turned and looked at the people. She saw their frightened, tired faces, and she felt compassion for them. At last she spoke. "I will ask the river to return to you," she said. "But just as the river gives water to all who are thirsty, no matter who they are, so you must learn to treat everyone with kindness, even those who seem different from you."

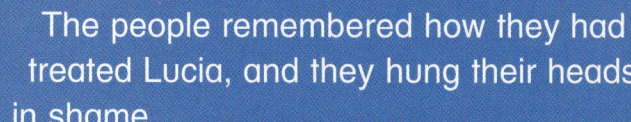

The people remembered how they had treated Lucia, and they hung their heads in shame.

Seeing that the people were truly sorry for what they had done, Lucia returned with them to the village and began to comb out her hair. She combed out the water, she combed out the fishes, she combed out the otters, and she kept on combing until the river had returned once more to where it belonged.

The people were overjoyed to have their river again. They poured water over themselves and over their animals, they jumped into the river, and they laughed and cried with happiness.

In all the excitement, no one noticed at first that Lucia had disappeared again. When the children asked the Elders where she had gone, the Elders replied that Lucia had not really left them. Though they would not be able to see her, she would always be there, guiding and protecting them, helping them to live with love and understanding in their hearts.

Reflect on

Strategies: How did using the strategies you learned in this unit help you understand the story? What other strategies did you use?

Critical Literacy: What messages do you think the author wanted you to understand after reading this legend?

LIGHT

Science

In this unit, you will
- ask yourself questions while you read
- ask questions to gather information when you listen
- use formal and informal voice in your writing
- identify characteristics of PowerPoint presentations
- read charts and diagrams
- learn about light

LET'S TALK

Open Your Eyes to Light!

Find at least 15 sources of light in this picture.

Understanding reading strategies

Questioning
Asking questions makes you an active reader and helps you understand what you are reading.

Where Does Light Come From?

Shut your eyes tight—all you can see is darkness. Now, open your eyes again. If it is daytime, you will see that light is all around you.

Natural Light

Anything that gives off a light that we can see is called a light source. The light sources that are not created by people are called natural light sources. They include the sun, the stars, and lightning. During the day, the rays of the sun light up the earth. At night, if there are no clouds, you can see the stars twinkling in the sky. During thunderstorms, you might see different kinds of lightning.

→ Ask questions to check your understanding. What is a natural light source?

44 Light

NEL

There are other sources of natural light, too. Fireflies are insects that give off a pale, greenish-yellow light that flashes or glows in the dark. Deep down in the sea, some fish are able to produce flashes of light in the darkness. And, if you live in the northern or southern regions of the world, you can see the aurora, a dazzling display of coloured lights that flicker in the sky at night.

Ask questions about things you wonder about. How do some deep-sea fish produce light? Sometimes the answer is not in the text.

Artificial Light

There are also many light sources that don't occur naturally but are created by people. These are called artificial sources of light. Electric lights, oil lamps, and even candles are all artificial light sources. You can find your way in the dark by using a flashlight powered by batteries. Without artificial light, there would be no television or movies. And city streets are full of artificial lights—vehicle headlights, brightly coloured advertisements, streetlights, and neon lights.

Make a personal connection. Where else have I heard the word *artificial* used?

Uses of Light

Light does more than just enable us to see. We use beams of light to cut metals into complicated shapes or to perform surgery. Light even helps us to stay healthy. When sunlight shines on our skin, our body makes a vitamin called vitamin D, which helps our teeth and bones to grow healthy.

Ask questions to find information. How is light used? Did you find the information in the text?

What Does Light

by Sally Nankivell-Aston and Dorothy Jackson

Light travels better through some materials than others. Clear materials that let all light through are called transparent. Materials that let some light through, but not all, are called translucent. Materials that light cannot travel through at all are called opaque. Find out more in this activity.

Applying Strategies

Questioning
As you read, ask questions to:
- check your understanding
- find out about things you wonder about
- make personal connections
- find information

You will need
- assorted pieces of fabric
- a selection of other materials (such as a clear glass, thick cardboard, a metal tray, tissue paper, tracing paper, a plastic bag, a book, a piece of wood)
- a flashlight

TRAVEL THROUGH?

1. Look closely at the fabric and other types of materials. Predict what will happen when you shine a flashlight at each one. Which will let all the light through, which will let just some light through, and which will not let any light through at all?

2. Make a chart like this one and record your predictions on it.

Material	Prediction			Result
	transparent	translucent	opaque	

3. Now shine the flashlight at each material. Make sure you keep the distance between the flashlight and each material short (about 10 centimetres). Ask a friend to look at the other side of the material. Can your friend see the light shining through?

4. Record the results in the chart.

5. Now sort your materials into three groups: transparent, translucent, and opaque.

Keep Thinking

Have you noticed that the clouds in the sky sometimes get in the way of the sun's rays? Do you think clouds are transparent, translucent, or opaque?

Don't Stop There

Take the flashlight around your home or school and test some other items to find materials that are transparent, translucent, or opaque.

In Action

Sometimes we need to use translucent or opaque materials to block out some or all of the light. Net curtains and frosted or patterned glass are used to block out some light—and also to stop people from looking in!

Blackout curtains were used in World War II to make sure no light showed outside.

Reflect on

Strategies: What questions did you ask that really helped you understand what you were reading?

Critical Literacy: Why do you think the writers presented this information as an activity? Did the writers' presentation help you understand the information?

Understanding speaking and listening strategies

Asking Questions

Asking questions is a good way to check your understanding while you're listening. Most people are very happy to answer questions because it shows that their listeners are interested in what they are talking about.

How to ask questions:

- ☑ When you don't understand something, ask a question.
- ☑ When you want more information, ask a question.
- ☑ Make your question as clear as you can so the person you're questioning understands what you want to know.

Understanding writing strategies

Using Formal or Informal Voice

You use different "voices" every day when you talk with people. You probably use a formal voice when you are talking with most adults and an informal voice when you are talking with your friends. Writers use different voices, too. They choose the voice they think will help them connect with their audience.

Here are two articles about light pollution. As you read, think about the audience for each article.

SCIENCE A16

Light Pollution

Light pollution is a problem caused by too much artificial light shining in places where it is not wanted or needed.

In cities, light from streetlights, outdoor advertising, office buildings, airports, schools, and homes creates "sky glow," a hazy dome of light that blocks out the night sky.

More than half of the world's population can no longer see the Milky Way, a vast stretch of stars that has fascinated humankind for thousands of years.

Today, scientists are urging people to use "sky-friendly" lights. Sky-friendly lights direct light down to the ground where it is needed.

If people plan lighting carefully, the problem of light pollution can be solved.

Light pollution prevents star-gazing.

Formal voice is serious, factual, and free from personal comments. Formal writing is in complete sentences.

50 Light

EXPLORING THE SKY

HEY! TURN OUT THE LIGHTS!

The Milky Way

You've probably never heard of light pollution, but it's a big problem for millions of kids around the world—and you're probably one of them! What's light pollution? Light where you don't want it. It's that simple.

Every night, light from office buildings, advertising, airports, schools, and homes creates an ugly haze of light called "sky glow." And sky glow blocks out all the really cool things to see in the night sky, like stars and planets and even the Milky Way.

The good news is, we can get our night sky back. Good light planning and "sky friendly" lights that send light down—not up!—will do the trick. Then kids will be able to tune into the nightly star show, the longest running entertainment on the planet.

Informal voice is friendly, factual, and personal. Informal writing sounds like the writer is talking directly to the reader.

How to use formal or informal voice:

☑ Think about your audience. Choose the voice you think will connect with your audience.

☑ To write in a formal voice, be serious. Use facts. Write in complete sentences. Don't make personal comments.

☑ To write in an informal voice, be friendly. Use facts. Write as you would talk to a friend.

Facts of Light

by Lorraine Cameron

Applying Strategies

Reading Like a Writer

As you read, think about the voice the writer has chosen. Has the writer used a serious, factual voice or a friendly, informal voice?

Travelling Light Rays

To our human eyes, light travels in straight lines. Look at sunlight streaming through a window or shining through a group of trees. On a dark road, you can see how car headlights shine a beam of light that goes straight ahead. These narrow beams of light are called light rays.

On their own, light rays can't go around corners or curve themselves around objects in their way. But things can change the direction the beams are travelling in. Anything that crosses the path of a light ray—even air, water, or dust—affects how the light behaves.

When Light Is Reflected

Of the millions of things our eyes can see, only a few of them make their own light. The sun, stars, electric lights, fire, and fireflies are some examples. Most things that we can see do not make their own light. We can see them because they reflect light. When light rays hit something, some of them bounce off and scatter in all directions. When this reflected light enters our eyes, it allows us to see the shape and colour of the object.

Some objects reflect light better than others. How well an object reflects light depends on its surface.

The moon does not make its own light. We can see it because it reflects the sun's light.

The smooth, shiny pot reflects much more light than the black cast-iron pot.

Mirror, Mirror

What's special about a mirror? The shiny surface of a mirror reflects almost all of the light that hits it. The reflected light makes an image—a reflection—that matches the original almost perfectly. But you've probably noticed that a mirror image is actually a reversed copy of the original.

If you raise your left hand, your reflection will be raising its right hand!

Mirror Magic

Write something on a piece of paper and hold it up to a mirror. What do you see? Can you read it?

Try writing a message backward on a piece of paper. Hold it up to a mirror to read it. Have a friend stand behind you with another mirror. Use the mirror image in front of you to read your writing in the mirror behind you.

Sometimes, the surface of still water can produce a reflection almost as clear as a mirror. If something disturbs the surface, the light is reflected in different directions and makes the reflections blurry.

Reflect on

Writer's Craft: What voice did the writer use? Find a place in the article that helped you decide what voice the writer chose for this article.

Critical Literacy: How did the voice the writer used affect your reaction to the article?

Mr. Microscope's Reflections on Bike Safety

Interview by Annie Chan

Applying Strategies

Reading Like a Writer
As you read, think about whether the voice of the interview is formal or informal.

Jim Prall is a scientist who lives in my neighbourhood. He's nicknamed "Mr. Microscope" because he loves using a microscope. But he also loves his bike. I see him biking around all the time and it's *really* hard not to notice him! I decided to ask him about all his safety equipment.

Annie: Mr. Microscope, some of the neighbours say you are a bike safety nut.

Mr. M.: I am! I live in a big city and I share the road with drivers, pedestrians, and other cyclists. Riding my bike is fun, but I don't want to have an accident.

Mr. Microscope bikes to work for exercise.

Annie: Would you tell me about your vest, please? How does it keep you safe?

Mr. M.: My big idea is that it's important for drivers to see me. Drivers are looking at so many things on the road. But when they spot my bright orange vest with the big yellow X, they think, "Oh, there's a cyclist." Cyclists should always wear brightly coloured clothing.

Annie: How does your vest help you at night?

Mr. M.: Reflection! The yellow X works as a reflector. It's made of special reflective material. When car headlights hit the X, the light bounces right back to the driver. That way, drivers know where I am.

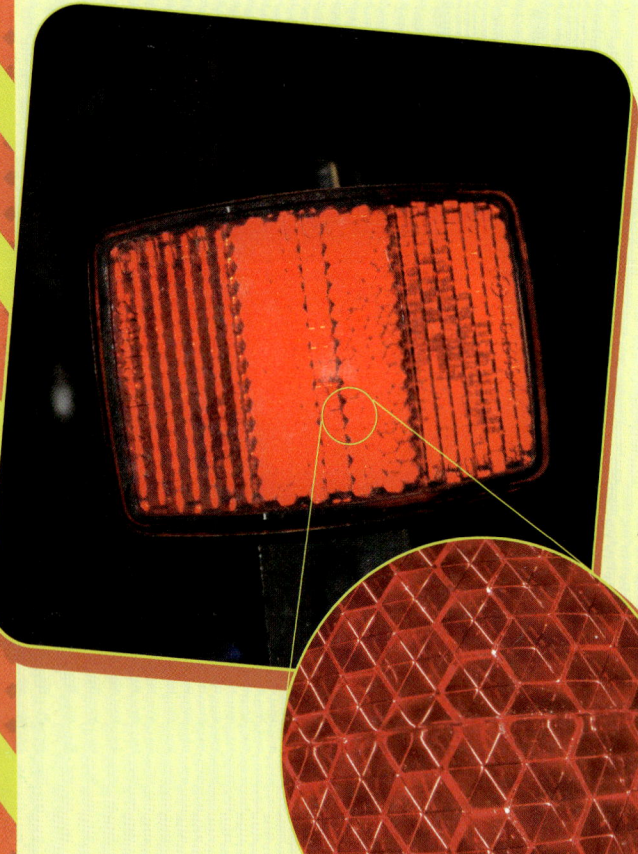

Annie: How do reflectors work?

Mr. M.: What's so cool about any kind of reflector is that it actually seems to shine. If you look closely at a reflector—under a microscope, maybe—you can see that it has thousands of tiny surfaces. At night, when light from a car hits a reflector, it bounces from one surface to another and then back to the car.

Annie: Do you have reflective material on your helmet too?

Mr. M.: Yep. I also have reflective tape on the back of my bicycle frame, on the front forks, and on my ankle straps. Plus all my backpacks have reflective tape on them. I attach a red flashing light on my back as well.

Annie: Last night I saw you with a headlight on your handlebars *and* a light strapped to your forehead! Why do you need both of them?

Mr. M.: Because two are better than one! They help me see where I'm going at night and they help drivers and other cyclists see me. I also have two bells on my bike, one for each hand.

Annie: Why do you have a mirror on your bike?

Mr. M.: The mirror lets me see cars and bikes coming up behind me.

Annie: Thanks for telling me your ideas about bike safety, Mr. Microscope.

Mr. M.: It was fun bouncing around ideas with you. I was happy to throw a little light on the subject.

Annie: Those are pretty bad jokes, Mr. Microscope.

Mr. M.: After a bit of *reflection*, I have to agree with you.

Reflect on

Writer's Craft: Find a place in the interview that helped you decide whether the voice was formal or informal.

Critical Literacy: How did the voice affect your enjoyment of the interview?

Understanding reading strategies

Text Features: Diagrams, Captions, and Charts

Diagrams, captions, and charts are text features. They can help you understand what you are reading by giving you additional information and by giving you visual information.

A caption tells you what is important about a diagram. How does this caption help you read the diagram? →

The Colours of Light

When we look at a beam of sunlight, it appears to travel through the air in a straight line. But when it enters another substance, such as water or glass, it changes direction. This bending of light is called refraction.

Sunlight is made up of many colours. Usually, the colours combine and look white. Sunlight bends when it passes through water droplets. The bent sunlight splits into all the colours of light—red, orange, yellow, green, blue, indigo, and violet.

A diagram shows how something works. What does this diagram show you? ↓

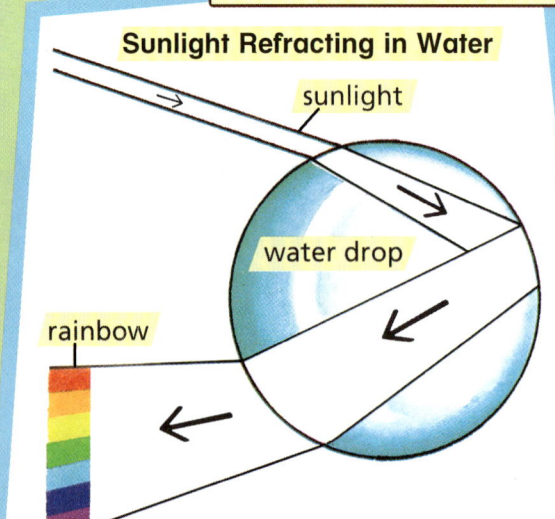

Sunlight Refracting in Water

Sunlight bends as it enters the edge of a drop of water. It is then reflected off the back of the drop and is bent again as it leaves the drop.

58 Light

A beam of light bends as it passes through a glass prism. The light splits into the colours of the rainbow.

A caption tells you what is important about a photograph. What does the caption tell you about this photograph?

Sunlight also splits into colours when it shines through a glass object called a prism. A prism bends sunlight into its rainbow colours, just as a water droplet would do!

When the sun is shining and it is raining at the same time, the raindrops split the sunlight into different colours.

Because different colours of light bend more than others, the bent sunlight forms an arch of the colours—a rainbow! This chart shows the order of the colours of a rainbow. Red light bends the least and is closest to being a straight line. Violet light bends the most. The order of colours in a rainbow never changes.

sunlight + raindrops = rainbow

Rainbow Colours	
Order	How They Bend
red	
orange	
yellow	
green	
blue	
indigo	
violet	

A chart is a way to organize information. The title tells you what the chart is about. The headings show you how the information is organized.

Written by Sheilah Currie
Illustrated by Helen Flook

Applying Strategies

Text Features: Diagrams and Charts

As you read, use text features to help you understand what you are reading.

- A diagram helps you understand how something works.
- A chart's title tells you what it's about. The headings show you how the information is organized.

My Aunt Stella has a great job. She's a senior scientist for a large, alternative-energy company. Last week, she sent an experiment for my brother and me to do. She made it sound like a riddle.

"Hmm," I mused. "It's something that will *guide you* out of the dark."

"I KNOW!" yelled my brother. "We could use a flashlight! That's what I'd use to get out of the dark!"

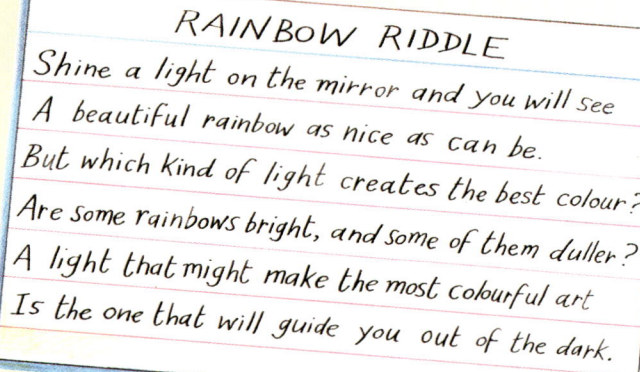

RAINBOW RIDDLE
Shine a light on the mirror and you will see
A beautiful rainbow as nice as can be.
But which kind of light creates the best colour?
Are some rainbows bright, and some of them duller?
A light that might make the most colourful art
Is the one that will guide you out of the dark.

It seemed like a reasonable idea, but first, we set up our materials the way Aunt Stella showed us in her diagram.

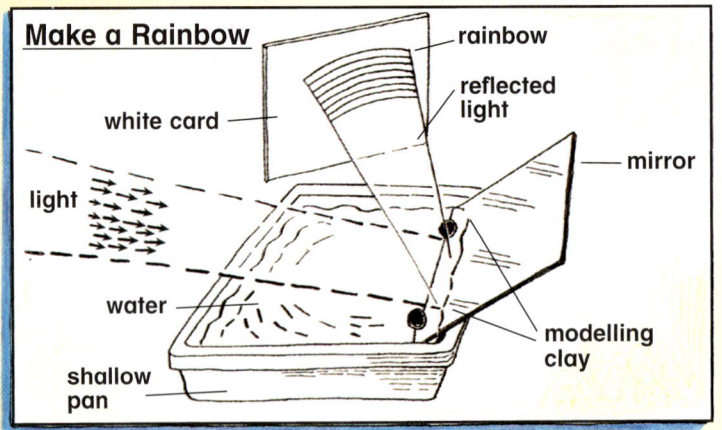

Make a Rainbow

We shone a flashlight on the mirror and held up the white card, but there was only a teensy bit of colour at the edge of a white glow.

My brother was disappointed, but then he got another idea. "A candle! Let's use a candle! That's what guided people out of the dark in the old days!"

I had to admit that a candle might be the answer, so we asked our dad to help us. When we tried the candle, though, our results were almost the same as with the flashlight. "Hmm," I wondered, "What else would 'guide you out of the dark'?"

We tried a couple of other kinds of light, but they just made teensy patches of colour. We were stumped and it was bedtime, so we decided to think up some other ideas the next day. Before I went to sleep, I made a chart of all the things we tried. I wanted Aunt Stella to know that we were being very *scientific*.

When my brother and I woke up in the morning, we were stunned. How could we have forgotten the most important source of light?

The sun! It was shining onto our mirror, and a beautiful rainbow appeared.

I guess we were *guided* out of the dark! Groan. Our Aunt Stella is *so-o-o* clever!

Making Rainbows	
Source of Light	Results
flashlight	round white reflection; dull colours; bit of colour around one edge
candle	flickering white reflection; dull; no colour
lamp	large white reflection; dull; bit of colour around one edge
mini book light	small white reflection; no colour; dull
sun	Rainbow! most colourful; order—red, orange, yellow, green, blue, indigo, violet

Reflect on

Strategies: How did text features help you understand what you were reading?

Connections: When have you used a hands-on activity to help you solve a problem?

Understanding media

Identifying Characteristics of PowerPoint Presentations

The Wonder of Fireflies

PowerPoint is a software program you can use to create reports. PowerPoint lets you use text, pictures, animation, and sound to share your learning with others in interesting ways.

Look at how these students used PowerPoint to tell about fireflies.

The opening slide tells the topic and the names of the creators. These students recorded themselves reading the title. They also made the fireflies blink on and off.

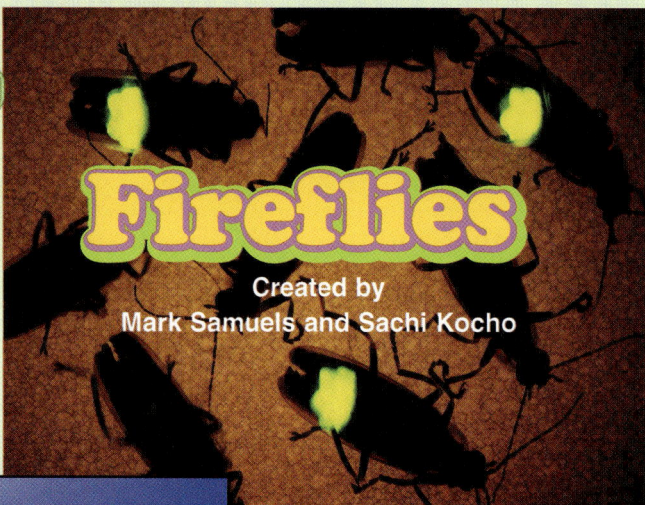

Fireflies
Created by Mark Samuels and Sachi Kocho

- What are fireflies?
- Where do fireflies live?
- Interesting firefly facts

The next slide lists the main sections in the report. The students used a font that is easy to read. The type is yellow and the background is dark to make viewers think of fireflies at night.

What are fireflies?
- Fireflies are actually a kind of beetle.
- Some people call fireflies "lightning bugs."
- A firefly's body uses chemicals to make a glowing light that blinks.
- About 125 different kinds of fireflies are found in North America.

Pyralis Firefly

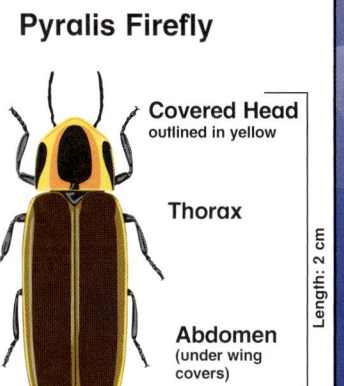

- Covered Head (outlined in yellow)
- Thorax
- Abdomen (under wing covers)

Length: 2 cm

Diagrams, maps, and photographs help the viewer understand the topic. Text explains what is important to notice in these visuals.

Where do fireflies live?

Fireflies can be found across southern Canada, from British Columbia to Québec.

Fireflies usually like damp places, such as fields or lawns, or the edges of woods and streams.

Interesting firefly facts

- Fireflies glow to attract a mate.
- Each kind of firefly blinks its light in a certain pattern.
- Fireflies may also glow to warn predators that they taste bad.

The last slide gives a strong ending to the report. These students added nature sounds to keep the viewer thinking about the wonder of fireflies.

Tips for Making a VIDEO

Written by Mark Shulman and Hazlitt Krog   Illustrated by Martha Newbigging

Putting It All Together

As you read this article, remember the strategies you've learned in this unit:

- Ask questions to help you understand what you are reading.
- Identify whether the voice is formal or informal.
- Use diagrams, captions, and charts to get additional information or visual information.

So, you'd like to wow your friends and family by making a video? Then you'll want to learn more about light!

Let There Be Lighting

Light is very important when you are making your own video. Here are some sources of light that should be handy to you when you're ready to videotape:

Built-in Light Some camcorders have a small built-in light. It's good for home movies, but not really good enough for your super-professional show.

Daylight The sun is great for light, but it's hard to move it where you need it. And the sun decides its own schedule. Good news: it's free and plentiful. Bad news: sunlight puts deep shadows on people's faces.

Indoor Lights Any of the lights in your house can help your shoot.

Work Lights Clip-on work lights are great because they are easy to point at your actors.

Types of Lighting

Let's take a look at some basic types of lights and their effect on videotape. Try not to mix them in a shot. And remember, consistent light is better than perfect light.

Kind of Light	What Is It?	What's It Good For?
Daylight	A brilliant golden light from our local star.	Exterior (outdoors) shooting in daytime, shooting inside rooms with lots of windows.
Halogen	A brilliant white light bulb found in many desk and floor lamps.	Everything ... halogen mixes pretty well with daylight, too.
Tungsten	The normal everyday light bulb. These regular light bulbs have a warm, yellowish light.	Interior (indoors) shooting when that's all that can be done; tungsten makes a video look "homey."
Fluorescent	A blue-white light from tube bulbs.	Shooting inside schools, stores, or bathrooms, where we expect that kind of light. Usually makes people look pale or cold.
Neon	Tubes filled with gas that can be shaped to spell words in different colours.	Establishing a mood or setting.

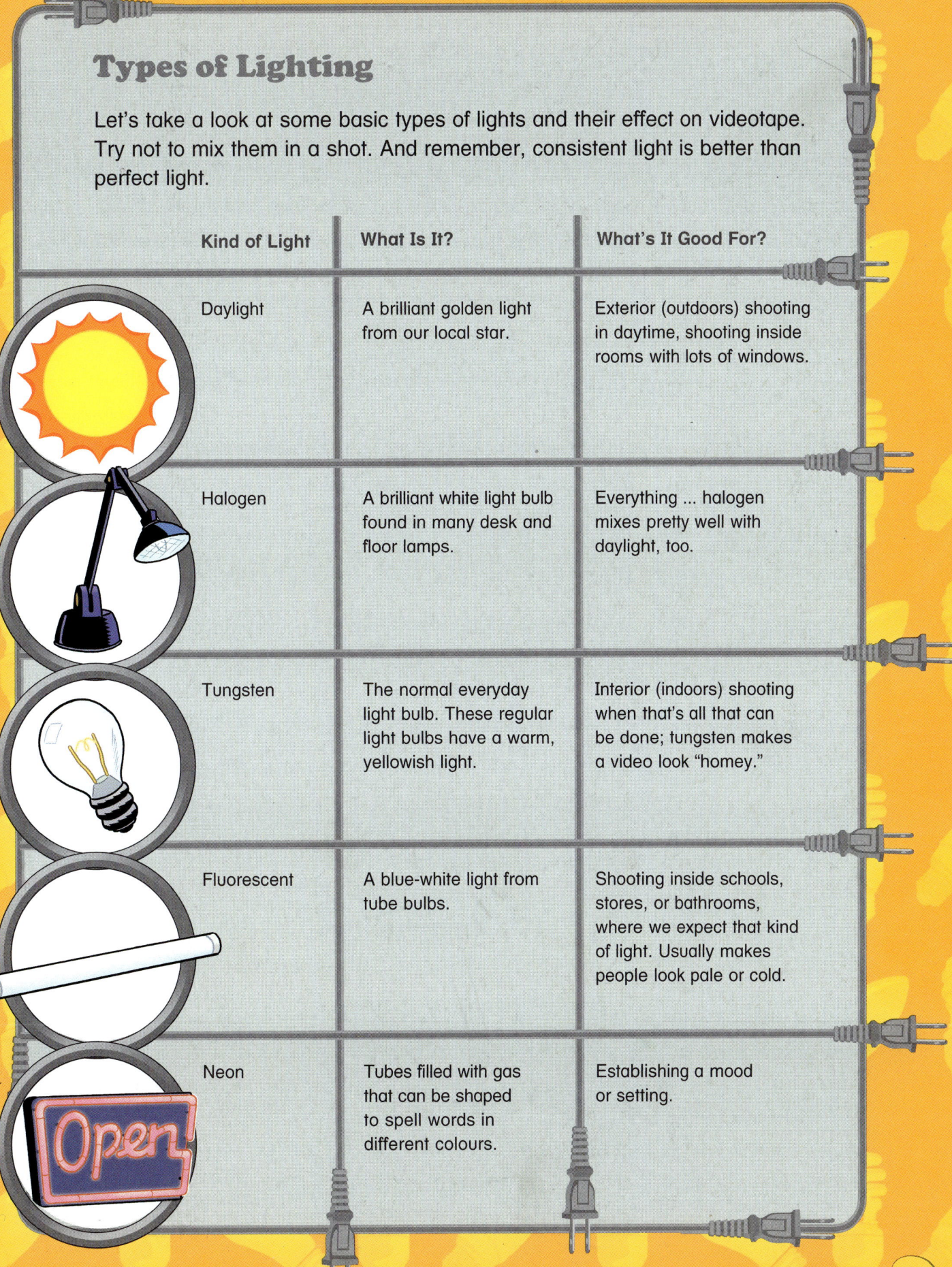

no light

key light

key light + fill light

key light + fill light + backlight

Light Like a Pro

Your best bet is to use existing light. (That means shooting your video where there is already lots of light.) But, if you want to learn lighting, here's how the professionals do it.

It's called **three-point lighting**: three lights in three different places aimed at the middle, and presto!—they almost erase each other's shadows. Hard shadows are bad stuff in videos, except in monster and bad-guy stories.

There are three kinds of lights in this system:

Key light—The first and brightest light, usually pointing at the subject. A work light, or a 100-watt bulb without a shade, would make a good key light.

Fill light—The second light, half as bright, is placed opposite the key light on the other side of the camera. It softens most of the shadows cast by the key light. A basic work light with a 50-watt bulb, or a lamp with a shade, can do the trick.

Backlight—The third light is set behind the talent (actors), to help them stand out from the background. Don't shine it directly into the camera lens. A lamp (with a shade) in the background would make a good backlight for you. You can even keep it visible in the frame.

If you can't get all three lights set up, try just a key and a fill light. No? Just a key light, then. No? Use the light on your camcorder. Or the sun. Or the refrigerator light....

Reflect on

Strategies: What strategies did you use when you were reading this article? Find a place in the article where you found yourself reading in a new way.

Your Learning: Which tips do you want to remember when you make a video?

Canada's Regions

In this unit, you will

- read maps
- summarize main ideas
- use sensory words in your writing
- identify characteristics of sequence text pattern
- identify conventions of postcards
- learn about Canada's regions

LET'S TALK

"Eh" Is for Canada

How many of these 20 Canadian things can you identify? Where in Canada do you think you might see each one?

Understanding reading strategies

Reading a Map

A map gives information about a place on Earth's surface. Maps can include lines, colours, pictures, symbols, and words.

A map has a title. What does the title of this map tell you? ↓

A Map of Canada's Regions and Resources

Words are used to label important places. What places are labelled on this map?

A compass rose shows direction. Which way is north on this map? →

70 Canada's Regions

Understanding reading strategies

Summarizing

A summary is a short statement of the main ideas in a piece of writing. Summarizing main ideas helps you to think about what is important and to understand and remember what you are reading.

→ Read the title and the beginning of the article. Stop to ask yourself, "What is this article about?"

→ Stop at the end of each section and identify the main idea. What is the main idea in this section?

THE CANADIAN SHIELD

by Susan Hughes

Canada is made up of many physical regions. One region found in the middle of the country is the Canadian Shield.

The Shield curves around Hudson Bay and covers more than one-third of Canada. It is a beautiful region—with sparkling lakes, rushing rivers, and rich forests—but underneath it all is rock. The rock is like a huge shield covering Earth.

ANCIENT BULLDOZERS

The Canadian Shield began as high mountains billions of years ago. Slowly, wind and rain wore the mountains down. At the same time, plants started to grow. Rivers flowed. Then the Ice Age came. Massive glaciers worked like bulldozers to scrape across the landscape, shave down trees, and dig out hollows. Over time, these hollows filled with water and forests grew again, but some large areas remained bare rock.

Canada's Regions

RICH GIFTS

The Canadian Shield's waters, forests, and rocks add up to great riches for Canadians.

For centuries, people have used the Shield's lakes, rivers, and streams for transportation. They have also fished in them for food. More recently, people have made power from the region's huge supply of water.

Canadians cut down the trees in the Shield's forests, then take them to sawmills and paper mills. There, the trees are made into pulp, paper, and lumber products.

Like a knight's shield, the rock of the Canadian Shield is made of valuable minerals. In fact, the region is one of the top mining areas in the world. Workers take minerals such as iron ore, copper, zinc, and nickel from the ground.

← Look for key words. What key words tell you about the main idea of this section?

These miners are drilling for gold in Ontario's bedrock.

RESOURCES AND COMMUNITIES

Canadians have been attracted to the many resources of the Canadian Shield. They have built mines, mills, and hydroelectric plants—and built communities in which to live.

Look at this map. It shows some of the many **communities in the Canadian Shield that have grown because of the Shield's rich natural resources: water, forests, and rocks.**

Each section → has a main idea. What is the main idea in this section?

Summarizing What You've Read

After you've finished reading, think back to remember the main ideas. You can summarize the main ideas by saying them to yourself, or by making a visual organizer like this one.

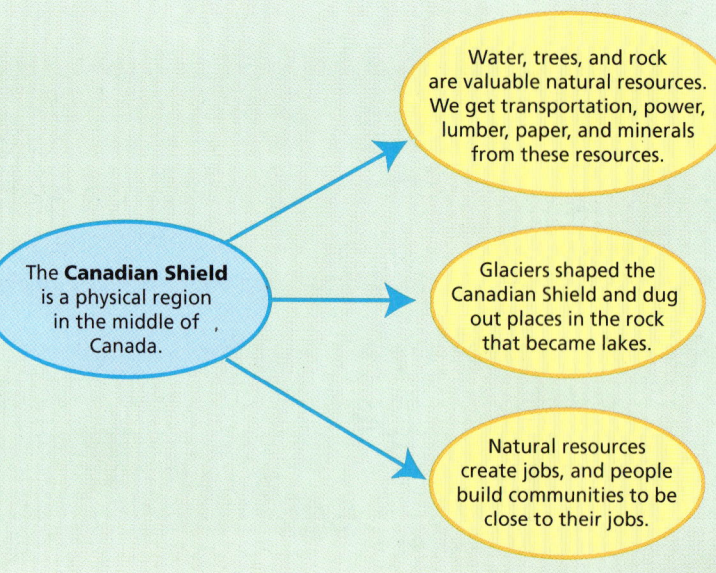

THE INTERIOR PLAINS

by Susan Hughes

Applying Strategies

Summarizing

As you read, remember the steps for summarizing:

- Read the title and beginning of the article.
- Stop at the end of each section and identify the main idea.
- Look for key words.
- Use a visual organizer to summarize the main ideas.

Canada's Interior Plains

Imagine an ancient sea covering most of the Northwest Territories, most of Alberta, and plenty of Saskatchewan and Manitoba.

Over time, wind and rain wear away at the rocky land east of the sea. It becomes sand, silt, and mud, which settles in the sea bottom.

More time passes. The climate changes. The water in this sea dries up. The bottom of the sea is now the surface of Earth. Dinosaurs prowl the landscape.

The Ice Age buries the region under thick glaciers. When these moving masses of ice finally melt away, what is left behind? The resource-rich lands of Canada's Interior Plains.

These hoodoos are in the Badlands, in southern Alberta. Many were formed when glaciers melted. When water rushed past, the layers of hard rock did not erode but the softer surrounding rock did.

Flat—and More

When you think about Canada's Interior Plains, do you picture a landscape as flat as a pancake? Much of the region *is* flat. However, the landscape is varied. It includes the following:

- plateaus—large flat areas that are higher than the surrounding land
- lowlands—large flat areas that are lower than the surrounding land
- cliffs and escarpments—steep connections between flat areas at different heights
- hoodoos—rock shaped like chimneys
- rolling hills—some are called "foothills" because they are at the "feet" of the nearby Rocky Mountains

Home, Home on the Plain

Today, the Interior Plains makes use of its long history. Canadians discovered that the rocks that were once at the bottom of the ancient sea contain coal, oil, and gas. People now use these resources to make important fuels, such as gasoline and home-heating oil.

On top of the ancient seabed is some of the best farmland in the world. Farmers grow wheat, oats, and barley and raise farm animals.

And now visitors come for the region's parks, lakes, and rivers—and dinosaurs.

Reflect on

Strategies: Think about what you do when you are summarizing main ideas. Why is this useful to you as a reader?

Your Learning: What have you learned that would help you enjoy a trip to the Interior Plains?

Canada's Regions

Understanding Writing Strategies

Using Sensory Words

Writers use sensory words when they want to create a picture in their readers' minds. Sensory words tell what you want your reader to see, hear, feel, smell, and taste.

You can brainstorm a word bank of sensory words before you begin writing. Can you imagine two very different places by reading these two word banks?

I see	I hear	I feel	I smell	I taste
towering pines	rushing water	rough bark	fresh air	wild raspberries
fallen logs	hooting	chilly breeze	rotting leaves	
speedy squirrels	crunchy pine needles	scratchy scarf	pine	

I see	I hear	I feel	I smell	I taste
foamy shore	waves crashing	hot	sunscreen	salt
big waves	laughter	sweaty	hot dogs	cool drink
bright umbrellas	loud music	gritty, sandy	wet towels	lip balm

How to use sensory words:

✓ Picture in your mind what you want to write about.

✓ Make a word bank and brainstorm as many sensory words as you can.

✓ Read your words out loud. Think about how these words will help your readers to create a picture in their minds. Use the words that make the best picture.

✓ Add new words as you write!

The Seas We

Written by Robert Heidbreder
Illustrated by Claire Fletcher

Applying Strategies

Reading Like a Writer
As you read, look for the sensory words the poet uses to create word pictures.

Won't you see the sea I see?
Come and see the sea by me.

See the sea that I can see,
the Atlantic rolling free.

Won't you hear the sea I hear?
Pounding sounding loud and clear.

Hear the sea that I can hear,
the Pacific crashing near.

Won't you feel the sea I feel?
Freezing foaming at my heel.

share

Feel the sea that I can feel,
icy Arctic cold as steel.

Won't you smell the sea I smell?
Warm and golden earth seashell.

Smell the sea that I can smell,
waving grain in summer's spell.

And won't you taste the sea I taste?
The sea of wind around my face.

Taste and feel the sea of air,
smell, see, hear the seas we share.

Reflect on

Writer's Craft: How did thinking about sensory words help you enjoy this poem?

Connections: Think about a TV show or movie with an ocean setting. Which words in the poem remind you of this setting?

Fox on the Ice

Written by Tomson Highway
Illustrated by Brian Deines

Applying Strategies

Reading Like a Writer

As you read, imagine you are on the ice watching the story happen. The author uses many sensory words to help you see, hear, feel, smell, and taste the action.

Tomson Highway was born in northern Manitoba and his first language is Cree. He wrote this story in both Cree and English.

One winter afternoon, Joe and Cody went ice fishing with their papa, their mama, and Cody's little black dog, Ootsie. It was the perfect day to fish. The sky was clear, and the sun made the snow sparkle like diamonds.

It was also the perfect day for a picnic. The family ate a big lunch of bannock baked over a fire, broiled whitefish right out of the lake, and hot, smoke-flavoured tea. After lunch, the eight grey huskies dozed happily in the sun. Joe was also half asleep, cuddled up by his mother in the sled.

mahkesís mískwamíhk e-cípatapít

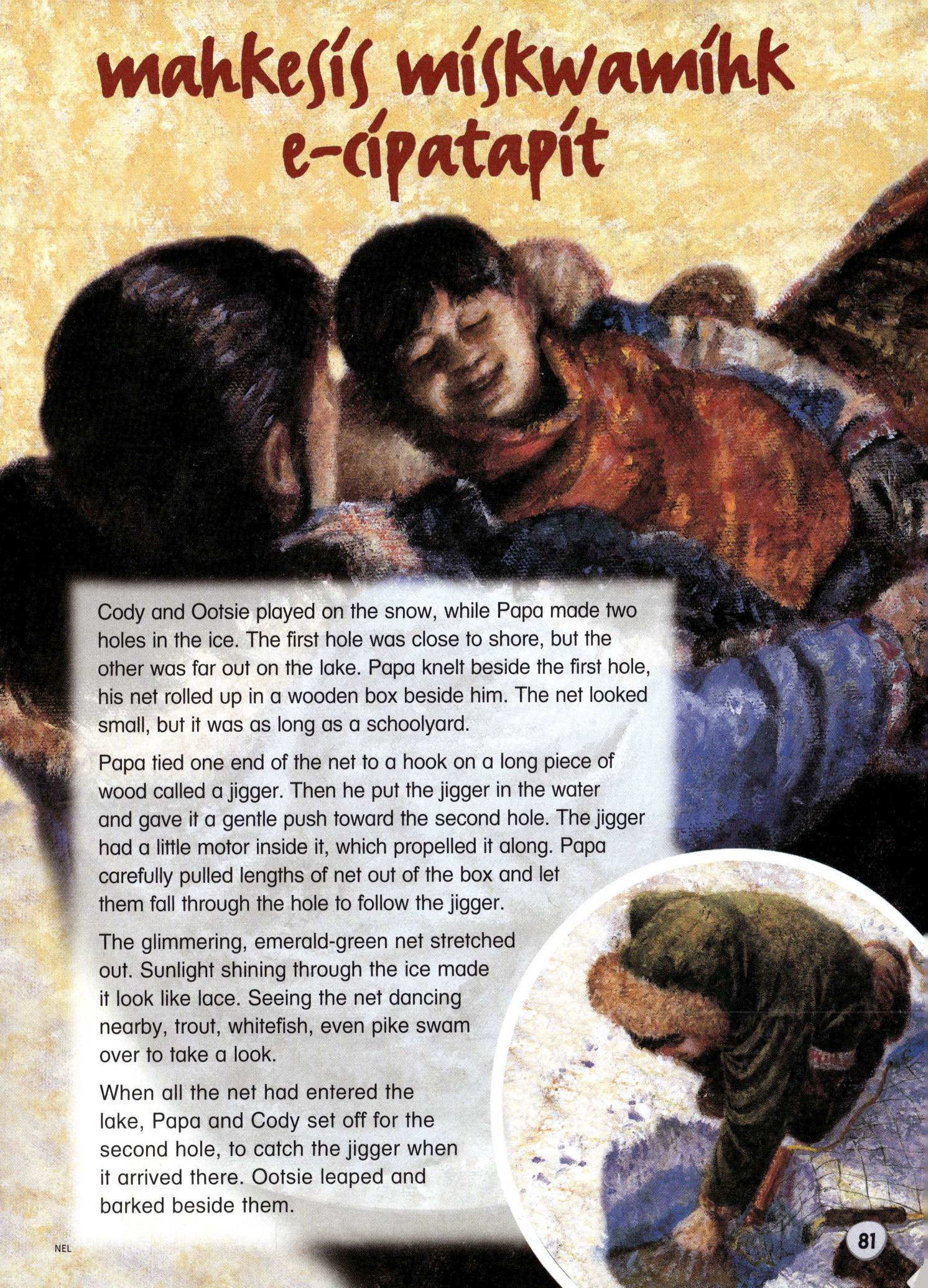

Cody and Ootsie played on the snow, while Papa made two holes in the ice. The first hole was close to shore, but the other was far out on the lake. Papa knelt beside the first hole, his net rolled up in a wooden box beside him. The net looked small, but it was as long as a schoolyard.

Papa tied one end of the net to a hook on a long piece of wood called a jigger. Then he put the jigger in the water and gave it a gentle push toward the second hole. The jigger had a little motor inside it, which propelled it along. Papa carefully pulled lengths of net out of the box and let them fall through the hole to follow the jigger.

The glimmering, emerald-green net stretched out. Sunlight shining through the ice made it look like lace. Seeing the net dancing nearby, trout, whitefish, even pike swam over to take a look.

When all the net had entered the lake, Papa and Cody set off for the second hole, to catch the jigger when it arrived there. Ootsie leaped and barked beside them.

Suddenly, the sled dogs woke up. They had smelled a stranger. On the other side of the lake sat a fox, her fur as bright as flames. She sat perfectly still, sniffing the delicious lunch smells that lingered in the air.

The huskies snarled and barked. They jumped to their feet and took off after the fox. The sled went with them. So did Joe and Mama.

The fox just yawned, shook herself, and wandered off. She didn't even give the dogs a second look.

Mama dug her heels into the snow on both sides of the sled to slow it down. Joe squealed with glee.

"Whoa!" Mama screamed to the dogs. "Whoa, whoa, whoa!" But the dogs didn't listen.

Jets of snow flew up from Mama's heels. Rainbows danced inside them. To Cody, the sled looked like a faraway angel taking off on wings of rainbow snow. Mama's shouts and the dogs' barks sounded like crystal chimes.

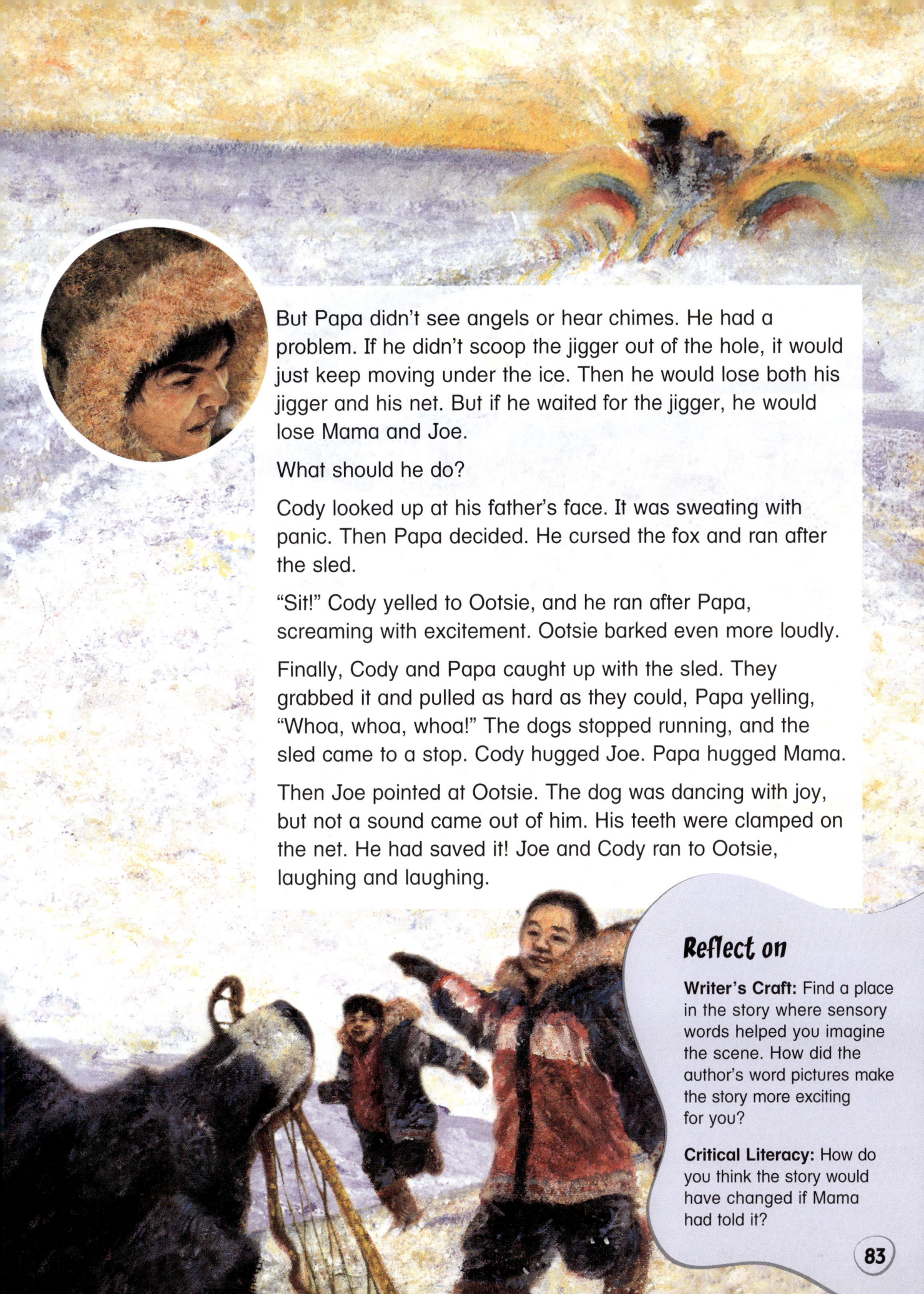

But Papa didn't see angels or hear chimes. He had a problem. If he didn't scoop the jigger out of the hole, it would just keep moving under the ice. Then he would lose both his jigger and his net. But if he waited for the jigger, he would lose Mama and Joe.

What should he do?

Cody looked up at his father's face. It was sweating with panic. Then Papa decided. He cursed the fox and ran after the sled.

"Sit!" Cody yelled to Ootsie, and he ran after Papa, screaming with excitement. Ootsie barked even more loudly.

Finally, Cody and Papa caught up with the sled. They grabbed it and pulled as hard as they could, Papa yelling, "Whoa, whoa, whoa!" The dogs stopped running, and the sled came to a stop. Cody hugged Joe. Papa hugged Mama.

Then Joe pointed at Ootsie. The dog was dancing with joy, but not a sound came out of him. His teeth were clamped on the net. He had saved it! Joe and Cody ran to Ootsie, laughing and laughing.

Reflect on

Writer's Craft: Find a place in the story where sensory words helped you imagine the scene. How did the author's word pictures make the story more exciting for you?

Critical Literacy: How do you think the story would have changed if Mama had told it?

Understanding text patterns

Identifying Characteristics of Sequence Text Pattern

When writers want to share information where the time order is important, they can use sequence text pattern. In sequence text pattern, events are presented in the order in which they happened.

A travel diary is an example of sequence text pattern.

Dates and time words help the reader to follow the order of events. When did Guy start writing his Ontario travel diary?

GUY'S ONTARIO

From *Wow Canada!* by Vivien Bowers

This summer, I'm travelling with my family to every province and territory in Canada. Here's part of my travel diary.

Manitoba-Ontario border

July 17, Day 8

Today we drove into Ontario, north of Lake of the Woods, and then drove and drove and drove! Will we ever get to the other side, though? Ontario is 1600 kilometres across.

Manitoba | Ontario

Day 8

Lake of the Woods

Thunder Bay — Day 9

Lake Superior Provincial Park

Lake Superior

Lake Michigan

I looked at the map, and I think it's also bigger than it's supposed to be from top to bottom. From the west, the border between Canada and the United States follows neatly along the 49th parallel of latitude—but Ontario's border goes berserk! At Point Pelee, in Lake Erie, the border drops way down south—so far that cactuses grow there!

84 Canada's Regions

ADVENTURE

July 18, Day 9

Thunder Bay

Rachel, Mum, Dad, and I spent the day at Old Fort William, a big fur-trading post in what is now Thunder Bay. We were time-warped back to the year 1815, and helped a voyageur who was building a birchbark canoe. He told us he paddles 16 to 18 hours a day. Rachel thought that was nuts.

"Haven't you heard of speedboats?" she asked.

Tonight, we're camping at Lake Superior Provincial Park. Tomorrow, we'll drive and drive to Lake Huron—another Great Lake.

← Print and text features can help the reader understand the sequence. What does this heading tell you about where Guy was on July 18th?

← Visuals help the reader understand the order of events. Use the map to see which park Guy visited first—Killarney Provincial Park or Lake Superior Provincial Park.

According to Dad

Since we keep talking about the Great Lakes, Rachel and I asked Dad what was so <u>great</u> about them. He told us they are five linked lakes, the biggest in a chain of large lakes along the southern border of the Canadian Shield. They are Lake Superior, Lake Michigan (which is entirely in the United States), Lake Huron, Lake Erie, and Lake Ontario. Since the early days of the fur trade, the Great Lakes have provided an important transportation route into the North American continent. They drop from 183 metres above sea level at Lake Superior to 74 metres at Lake Ontario. The most dramatic drop is at Niagara Falls (stay tuned—we're heading there soon!).

July 20, Day 11

Killarney Provincial Park

Today, we went for a (wet) canoe trip in Killarney Provincial Park. We had to do a portage, which means carrying the canoe on our shoulders, which I do not recommend. Not ever, but especially not when the trail is muddy and slippery.

On our canoe ride, I saw a moose and some monarch butterflies, so I added them to my wildlife list. Rachel collected a poison ivy rash, which she has to put cream on three times a day.

July 22, Day 13

Georgian Bay

We're staying for a few days at our friends' cottage on the French River, near Georgian Bay, on the north shore of Lake Huron.

We were happy to get to our friends' cottage. We spent all day swimming and jumping off rocks.

The weather has been perfect, but if it turns bad we have a rainy-day plan. We'll go to Sudbury for a day. We can visit Science North, which is supposed to be a cool science museum, and the nickel mine.

Now I'm off to hit the sack. From my bed at night, I can hear the loons calling.

← Time words help the reader follow the order of events. When does Guy listen to the loons?

Niagara Falls

July 26, Day 17

The falls at last! Here's my e-mail to my friend Kyle.

> A letter or an e-mail can be written in sequence text pattern. How did Guy spend his day in Niagara Falls?

To: Kyle

From: Guy

Hey, Kyle!

This morning, we saw Niagara Falls from above, from behind, and even from a boat at the base of the falls. So many exciting ways to get soaked!

The falls look just like that photo in our social studies textbook. In fact, I kept thinking maybe I was looking at that photo, except for the thundering sound of crashing water and the fact that I spent the day soaking wet.

There are really two sets of falls, the Canadian Falls and the American Falls. The Canadian Falls are bigger (this must annoy the Americans) and curve in a horseshoe shape.

We spent the afternoon watching freighters go through the locks on the Welland Canal. Ships can travel all the way through the Great Lakes, but between Lake Ontario and Lake Erie it gets tricky. That's where Niagara Falls is. The freighters can bypass the falls, but they still have to get over that darned cliff called the Niagara Escarpment. To do this, they "climb" almost 100 metres through the canal's eight locks. That makes the Welland Canal the tallest water staircase in the world. It's one of the world's greatest engineering feats, according to the brochure.

We're going to Ottawa tomorrow. I'll say hi to the prime minister for you.

Later,

Guy

P.S. Wait till you see my photos!

POW

Nance Ackerman is a photographer who has been taking pictures around the world for many years. One of her favourite events to photograph is the powwow. Her love of powwows started with her Mohawk grandmother. This account tells about her taking photographs for a magazine article on powwows.

One summer, Nance packed up her cameras, lenses, and rolls and rolls of film. Then she travelled from her home in Nova Scotia to Saskatchewan—to a place about 100 kilometres southeast of Regina. As soon as she arrived, she carefully unpacked all her equipment and got ready to enjoy the Carry the Kettle First Nation Powwow!

The opening event was the grand entry procession. The participants came together, dancing and singing to the drummers' music. During the grand entry, Nance photographed the Chiniki Lake Singers performing the traditional opening song.

> **Applying Strategies**
>
> **Identifying Characteristics of Sequence Text Pattern**
> As you read,
> - Use visuals to help you understand the order of events.
> - Use text features, like captions, to help you understand the sequence.
> - Look for time words to help you follow the order of events.

The Chiniki Lake Singers from Morley, Alberta, perform the traditional opening song, "Heartbeat of a Nation."

WOW!

Written by Laura Edlund
Photographed by Nance Ackerman

Young dancers help each other get ready.

A teenage boy is dressed and waits his turn to perform.

After the grand entry, an Elder took Nance around and introduced her to many different people. She saw some young dancers getting ready for their performances. She took a picture of some boys helping each other with their outfits. Then she took a picture of a young man who was dressed and ready for his performance.

Later in the day, Nance noticed a woman and a girl walking hand in hand in the prairie grass. Nance couldn't resist taking their photograph.

Two performers take a break from the busy events of the powwow.

A dancer's silhouette shows in the light of the setting sun.

Over two days, Nance watched and photographed many daytime events of the powwow. When evening came, she found there were still more reasons to keep her camera ready. As the light changed with the setting sun, she took more pictures.

After sunset, and late into the evening, the powwow performances continued. Inside a large, lighted tent, Nance watched and photographed more dances. She wished that her photographs could show the music and singing, too!

Dancers perform later in the evening inside a tent.

A few days later, Nance was back home in Nova Scotia. She developed her film, sorted through her many photos, then chose some to send to the magazine's offices.

After that, she looked at some photographs she'd taken at another powwow. One of them showed jingle dancers. Nance thought that readers would be interested in learning that the jingle dance is performed by women in powwows all over North America, but that it started in an Ojibwa village in Ontario. Finally, she put all the photos she'd chosen in a package and sent it off to the magazine editors.

ANOTHER TRIP, ANOTHER POWWOW

Jingle dancers join in the grand entry procession at the Echoes of a Proud Nation Powwow in Québec.

At last, a year after Nance went to the powwows, 16 of her photos appeared in the July/August issue of *Canadian Geographic*. Her photographs made it possible for thousands of readers to share her passion for powwows.

Reflect on

Strategies: How does thinking about sequence text pattern help you understand what you are reading?

Connections: What important traditions have you learned about in your family? What pictures would you include in a photo essay about your traditions?

Identifying Conventions of Postcards

Send a Postcard!

Postcards have been a popular way of sending messages for over a hundred years. Postcards tell about faraway places and about the adventures of people who visit them. How do these small cards carry such big messages?

Postcards often show something special about a place and its culture. Why might this postcard make someone excited to visit British Columbia?

Postcard photographs usually show a place at its best. What do you learn by looking at this postcard? What words would you use to describe the scene?

The back of a postcard sometimes gives more information. There is space for a message, a stamp, and an address. What kinds of messages do people write on postcards?

Look at these postcards. What messages do they give you about Canada? Which one would you like to receive—or send?

Confederation Bridge

By Truck to the North

Written by Andy Turnbull with Debora Pearson

Putting It All Together

As you read this book excerpt, remember to use the strategies you've learned in this unit:

- Read a map.
- Summarize main ideas.
- Recognize sequence of events.

Bill and TD are ready to roll.

Bill's Route

"All set, TD?" asks Bill. TD wags her tail eagerly and stands up in Bill's lap, resting her front paws on the steering wheel. TD's full name is "The Dog" and she rides with Bill Rutherford on all his trips.

Bill is a long-distance trucker. He is driving his 18-wheel tractor-trailer from Vancouver, British Columbia, all the way to Tuktoyaktuk, Northwest Territories.

Tuktoyaktuk is so far north that fruit trees and vegetable crops can't grow there. Each winter, truckers like Bill bring in most of the food. Bill loads up at food warehouses in Vancouver. He has a gigantic grocery list, with everything from apples and canned soup to potatoes and lettuce. Bill's truck carries enough groceries to last 500 people for a whole month!

The apples in Bill's truck grew in an orchard east of Vancouver. The potatoes have come all the way from Prince Edward Island.

It will take Bill four days of hard driving to reach Tuktoyaktuk. Before he sets out on his journey, he inspects his truck to make sure that everything is working properly. It is January, so Bill needs to be ready for bad weather and icy roads.

Bill heads north on the Trans-Canada Highway, through the mountains. Many trucks heading south carry huge logs. The logs are going to mills where they will be turned into newsprint, cardboard, toilet paper, and other products. These products will then be shipped to other parts of Canada.

Logs also travel by water to mills.

At night, Bill pulls into a truck stop. It is like a home away from home for long-distance truckers. They can eat at the restaurant, visit with other truckers, watch TV, and even take a shower. At bedtime, Bill heads back to the truck. He sleeps in a bunk in the cab and TD curls up in a soft, cozy box on the floor.

When Bill stops to repair his truck on a lonely stretch of road, TD goes for a walk to check out the smells. Bill works fast because it is −49 °C. Brrr!

Bill's first stop in the Northwest Territories is the town of Inuvik. He is eager to meet his customers again. He parks the trailer in a downtown lot and turns it into a store. He puts stairs at the side opening of the trailer and adds a door, like the kind on a house, to the opening. Inside he clips shelves to the walls and marks prices on a blackboard. Soon the first customers arrive. Many of them bring toboggans to haul their groceries home on the snow-covered roads.

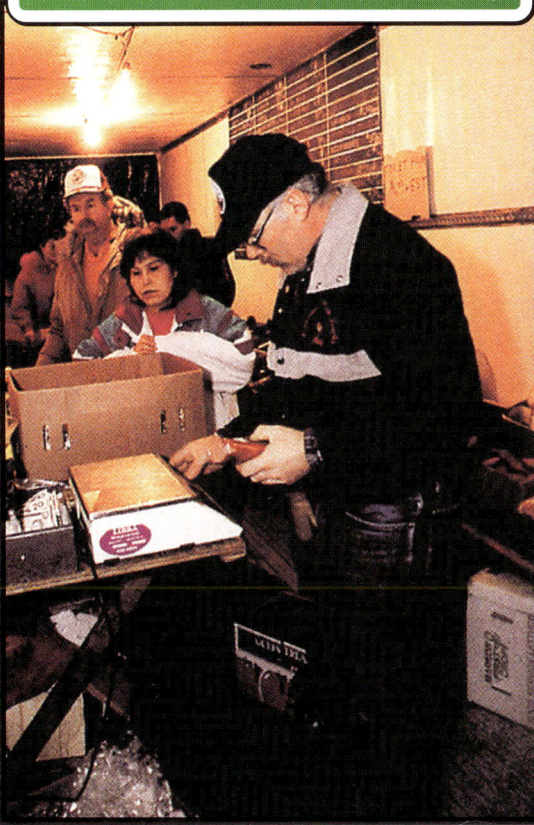

Bill uses a scale to weigh fruits and vegetables.

When customers walk up to Bill's "store" in Inuvik, this is what they see.

Bill's last stop is Tuktoyaktuk. The only way for him to get there is on an ice road. Every winter, snowplows clear ice roads across the frozen ocean, lakes, and rivers. These roads let northerners drive their cars, vans, and pickup trucks to other communities—something they can't do the rest of the year.

Planes take goods to the Arctic in every season, but flying goods north is more expensive than trucking them.

In winter, everything from lumber to lemons travels by truck on the ice roads. The ice makes cracking and popping noises as Bill's truck drives over it.

The people of Tuk really appreciate Bill's fresh produce from the south. After he has sold the last of his goods, Bill stands outside his truck to watch the northern lights dancing across the sky. At first, TD barks at the hissing and crackling sounds they make, but then she stops and seems to listen, too. Tomorrow Bill and TD will begin their long journey back to Vancouver.

In summer, the only way to get goods to Tuktoyaktuk is to fly them in.

Reflect on

Strategies: Which strategy do you think was the most useful in helping you understand this book excerpt? Try to think of two reasons why you picked this strategy.

Critical Literacy: This book excerpt provides information about transporting fresh food to Canada's north in the wintertime. Why do you think the authors included Bill and TD in their writing?

SOUND

Science

In this unit, you will

- identify characteristics of question-and-answer text pattern
- monitor your comprehension
- make your meaning clear while speaking
- identify point of view in web articles
- use strong verbs in your writing
- learn about sound

LET'S TALK

Sound Check

Can you find at least 30 sources of sound in this picture?

Understanding reading strategies

Monitoring Comprehension

Monitoring comprehension means checking to make sure you understand what you are reading. When you get stuck, you can use fix-it strategies to help you make sense of what you're reading.

→ Important words are often repeated. Make sure you understand important words. What do you know about vibrations?

A World Full of

by David Louis Dreier

Everywhere we go, there are sounds. We might hear people talking, dogs barking, or cars passing by in the street. Even the leaves on a tree make a sound as they rustle in the breeze.

It would be a much different world without sound. Imagine a world of complete silence. There would be no loud conversations among friends, no music, no alarm clocks.

But what is sound? What happens when a glass bottle breaks or a bird chirps that allows us to hear it?

What Is Sound?

Sound is produced by vibrations. When you talk, your vocal cords vibrate. A violin string, a radio, and a cricket all make their sounds through vibrations. These vibrations release energy. The energy moves away from the sound source (such as the radio) in the form of invisible waves.

104 Sound

Sound

You can see some kinds of waves. When you drop a stone into still water, the stone creates waves that move away from the centre of the splash. Sound waves also spread outward from a source of vibration.

When the waves reach us, they cause vibrations inside our ears. The vibrations cause signals that go to our brains.

> To figure out new concepts, use information in photographs. How does the photograph help you understand waves?

How It Works

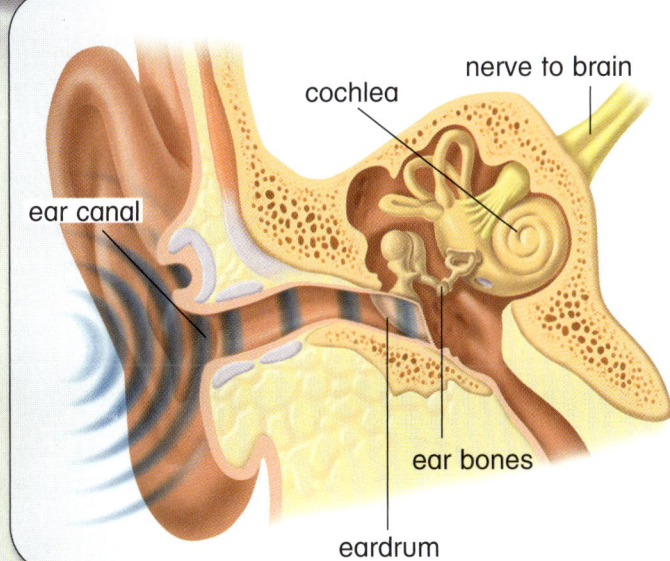

Sound waves enter the ear and hit the eardrum. This passes vibrations along three tiny bones to the curly shaped cochlea. The vibrations shake thousands of microscopic hairs inside the cochlea. These send nerve signals to the brain, which then identifies the sound.

> Look closely at word parts to help you figure out unfamiliar words. What smaller words do you recognize in the highlighted words?

> To understand a new concept, read ahead to find examples. How do the examples help you understand the concept of loudness?

> To understand a new concept, read ahead to find more information. Why does a loud sound seem less loud if it's far away?

Loud and Soft

The loudness of a sound is the amount of energy the waves are carrying. A friend's whisper or a cat's purr are soft sounds, with very little energy. An explosion creates a very loud sound because a great amount of energy has been released.

Of course, a loud sound doesn't seem loud if it is far away. That is because as sound waves move away from a source, their energy gets spread over a larger and larger space. The sound of someone humming right next to you might seem quite loud. At that close distance, most of the energy in the sound waves would be reaching your ears. But if you stood a little farther away, you might not even hear the humming.

Measuring Sound

The loudness of sound is measured in decibels (dB). This chart shows the decibel level of some everyday sounds. Loud sounds can damage our ears. Sounds louder than about 130 dB can make our ears hurt.

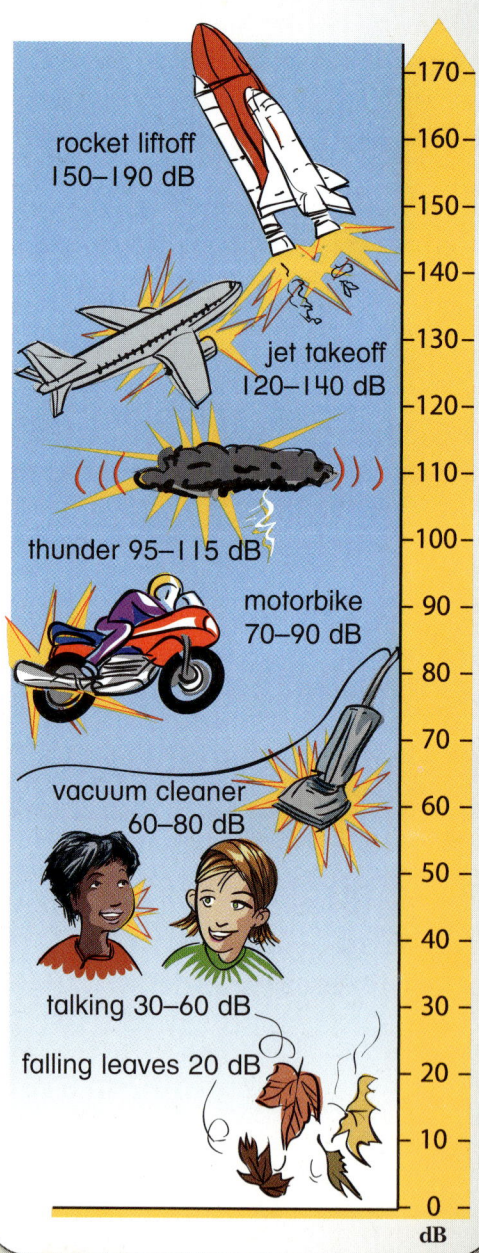

rocket liftoff 150–190 dB
jet takeoff 120–140 dB
thunder 95–115 dB
motorbike 70–90 dB
vacuum cleaner 60–80 dB
talking 30–60 dB
falling leaves 20 dB

BOUNCING BACK

by Barbara Taylor

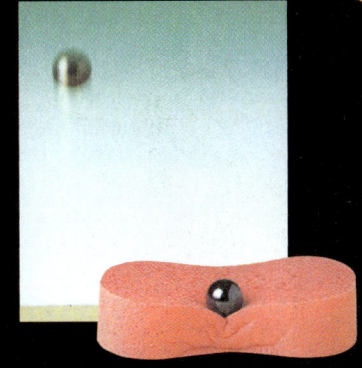

Try dropping marbles onto a hard surface and a soft surface. How is the sound different? When a sound hits a surface, it bounces back, or is reflected. Hard surfaces reflect sound better than soft surfaces. Soft surfaces soak up, or absorb, sounds so they do not bounce back as much. This makes sounds quieter.

In a concert hall, music bounces off the walls and ceiling. The materials in the walls and ceiling and the shape of the hall control the way the music bounces. Concert halls have to be carefully designed to cut down on unwanted echoes and make it possible for the audience to hear the music properly.

In concert halls, materials such as carpet, upholstered seats, and special tiles can help soak up sounds.

Applying Strategies

Monitoring Comprehension
As you read, check your understanding. Ask yourself if what you're reading is making sense. If you get stuck,

- make sure you understand important words
- use information in photographs
- read ahead to find examples and more information
- figure out unfamiliar words by looking at word parts

Bats make high, squeaking sounds and use their large, sensitive ears to collect the echoes from objects around them. This is called echolocation and helps bats to find their way around in the dark and detect food, such as insects. The echo-squeaks made by bats are usually too high for us to hear.

Try This

You will need
- an alarm clock
- a cookie tin with a lid
- tissue paper
- a towel

1. Place the ringing alarm clock inside the cookie tin and listen.
2. Put the lid on the tin and listen to the alarm again.
3. Wrap the clock in tissue paper inside the tin, put the lid on, and listen again.
4. Wrap the clock in a towel inside the tin, put the lid on, and listen to the alarm.

What did you notice about how the sound of the alarm changed? Which material worked best as soundproofing?

Reflect on

Strategies: Were there places you got stuck when you were reading this article? What strategies did you use to help you?

Your Learning: How does your school gym sound when you have an assembly? What did you learn in this article that you could use to change the sound in your gym?

Understanding writing strategies

Choosing Strong Verbs

Strong verbs help your readers visualize what you are writing about.

A weak verb gives a fuzzy picture. A strong verb lets your reader see, hear, smell, feel, and taste the action you are describing.

This student is writing about a sound he hears when he wakes up in the morning. What verbs does he choose? How does changing the verb help to make the picture in your mind clearer?

When the alarm ~~went off~~ sounded, I woke up.

When the alarm ~~sounded~~ rang, I woke up.

When the alarm ~~rang~~ clanged, I woke up.

When the alarm clanged, I woke up.

How to choose strong verbs:

☑ Picture in your mind what you want to write about.

☑ Brainstorm strong verbs.

☑ Ask yourself if the verbs match the picture in your mind.

☑ Try out other verbs to see if they are better.

SOUND THE ALARM!

People and animals use sound as an alarm. Sound can warn people of danger or remind them to do something important. An alarming sound is often very loud.

An alarm clock rings to let us know it is time to get up.
We might miss something important if we don't wake up.

Sirens wail to tell us that someone is hurt or in trouble and needs help.
Drivers of emergency vehicles turn on their sirens to let people know they are in a hurry.

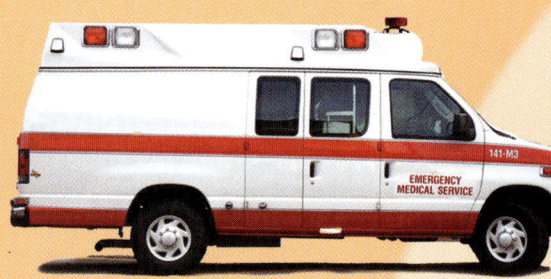

Lions roar to scare other animals away from their territory and food.
The roar lets other animals know they might become the lion's next meal if they come any closer.

Applying Strategies

Reading Like a Writer
As you read, look for strong verbs that help you hear the sounds in your mind.

Cats hiss, growl, and yowl when they feel angry or afraid.
Their sounds warn people and other animals to stay back. A hissing cat may attack.

Smoke alarms beep loudly to warn people that something may be burning nearby.
The alarm tells people to leave the building. They are in danger from smoke and heat.

Rattlesnakes rattle their tails to let other animals know they have come too close.
The snake's tail rattle warns others to go away or be bitten.

Slapping beaver tails alert other beavers to danger.
Beavers slap their broad tails against the surface of the water. This slapping sound can be heard both above and under water.

People yell to warn others about trouble.
Shouting for someone to "watch out" is a sound warning.

Reflect on

Writer's Craft: Find three verbs in the article that helped you hear the sound the writer was describing.

Connections: Think of a time when you heard an alarm. How did you feel? What did you do?

Applying Strategies

Reading Like a Writer

As you read, notice how the poet uses verbs to create pictures in your mind.

NOISE DAY

by Shel Silverstein

Let's have one day for girls and boyses
When you can make the grandest noises.
Screech, scream, holler, and yell—
Buzz a buzzer, clang a bell,
Sneeze—hiccup—whistle—shout
Laugh until your lungs wear out,
Toot a whistle, kick a can,
Bang a spoon against a pan,
Sing, yodel, bellow, hum,
Blow a horn, beat a drum,
Rattle a window, slam a door,
Scrape a rake across the floor,

Use a drill, drive a nail,
Turn the hose on the garbage pail,
Shout Yahoo—Hurrah—Hooray,
Turn up the music all the way,
Try and bounce your bowling ball,
Ride a skateboard up the wall,
Chomp your food with a smack and a slurp,
Chew—chomp—hiccup—burp.
One day a year do *all* of these,
The rest of the days—be *quiet* please.

Reflect on

Writer's Craft: If you were one of the "girls and boyses," what "grandest noises" would you like to make?

Critical Literacy: Do you think all boys and girls would enjoy a Noise Day? Who might not have fun on a Noise Day?

Understanding text patterns

Identifying Characteristics of Question-and-Answer Text Pattern

Question and answer is a way of organizing information. Each question introduces a topic and answers give information about the topic. Answers may include facts or explanations, or both.

FAQ: SOUND

by Etta Kaner

How do snakes hear without ears?

Snakes use the fact that sound travels better through solids than through air to "hear." Snakes have no ears, but if a snake lays its head on the ground, a bone inside its head picks up the sound vibrations coming from an approaching animal's movements. The vibrations travel to the snake's brain via a cochlea similar to the one inside the human ear.

Each question introduces a topic. What is the topic of this first question?

What's the quietest place in the universe?

Outer space. Sound must travel through air, liquid, or solids in order to be heard. In outer space, there is nothing to carry the sound waves. That's why astronauts must use radios to communicate. Radio waves can travel where sound waves cannot.

Answers give information about the topic. What information does this answer give you?

Does sound travel through water?

The next time you go swimming, ask a friend to tap two spoons or rocks under the water while your head is above the water. Can you hear anything? Now put your head under the water and try it again. Does sound travel through water? It sure does. In fact, it travels about four times faster through water than through air.

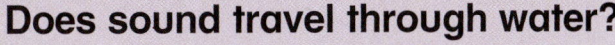 Answers may include facts. What do you learn about the speed of sound in water?

What's the noisiest animal in the world?

The male howler monkey of South America has two bony "sound boxes" in its throat. When it howls, air blows across the boxes, just like air blowing across empty pop bottles. The resulting roar can be heard over a distance of 5 kilometres.

How did Beethoven use his teeth to compose music?

Beethoven, a famous composer of the late 1700s and early 1800s, continued to compose great music even after he became deaf. To help him hear the music he was writing, Beethoven would hold one end of a wooden stick between his teeth and put the other end against the piano strings. When he played a note, the sound travelled through the stick, through his teeth and skull bones, directly to his inner ears.

Answers may give an explanation. What will be explained in the answer to this question?

Why is it so quiet just after a snowfall?

There are millions of tiny spaces inside and surrounding the flakes that make up the freshly fallen snow. These spaces absorb sound. This may be an advantage in a large city since it temporarily cuts down on noise pollution. But on Antarctic expeditions, people who are more than 5 metres apart in freshly dug snow tunnels must shout to be heard.

Can clothes change sound?

If music doesn't sound right in a concert hall, don't always blame the building's designer. The Royal Albert Hall in London, England, has been a popular place for concerts since 1871. But in the 1930s, people complained about the sound of the music there. Someone discovered that, since women were no longer wearing long dresses made of several layers of material, not as much sound was being absorbed. This problem was solved by adding special fibre tiles to the walls.

School of Sound

Interview by Laura Edlund

Bill Morgan is a judo competitor, a graduate of W. Ross Macdonald School in Brantford, Ontario, and now an educational assistant there. Bill has low vision, so he has learned to use sound to get around. He talked to us about sound and his school.

Applying Strategies

Identifying Characteristics of Question-and-Answer Text Pattern

As you read this interview, look for characteristics of question-and-answer text pattern:
- Each question introduces a topic.
- Answers give information about the topic.
- Answers may include facts or explanations, or both.

Laura: *What are some things that make your school great?*

Bill: The people who made the new school building had to figure out how it could work for the students. All the students at the school are blind or deafblind, or have low vision. Certain things at the school can help students get around independently. For example, the new school building has no carpets and has many wide hallways. These things help make the school great.

Bill Morgan has represented Canada in judo competitions around the world, including the Paralympics.

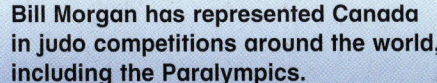

The school was established in 1872. This new school building was opened in 2004.

Laura: *Why aren't there any carpets?*

Bill: Well, for many students at the school, sound is information that can help them get around. Carpets muffle sound. But wood or tile floors reflect sound well and give information. Wide hallways with high ceilings reflect sound well, too. They don't create too many echoes, which can distort the information.

Laura: *What are other ways that some students use sound?*

Bill: Some students use certain sounds to figure out where they are in the school. For example, the hum of the vending machines or the sound of the water fountains can be a landmark for a student. Me? I can hear the doorways.

When Bill walks along hallways in the school, he hears the change in the sound reflected back to him. The sound reflected from a wall is different from the sound reflected through an open doorway.

Laura: *But how well can a student use sounds in a busy hallway?*

Bill: Sounds sure do get distorted when 100 students are walking in the halls. That's why we use the rule "Stay to the right!" And we use other sorts of information—for example, the rooms and hallways are in exactly the same place on each floor. That makes it easier for students to know where they are and to get where they are going. They can create a mental map of the school.

The school's motto is "The impossible is only the untried."

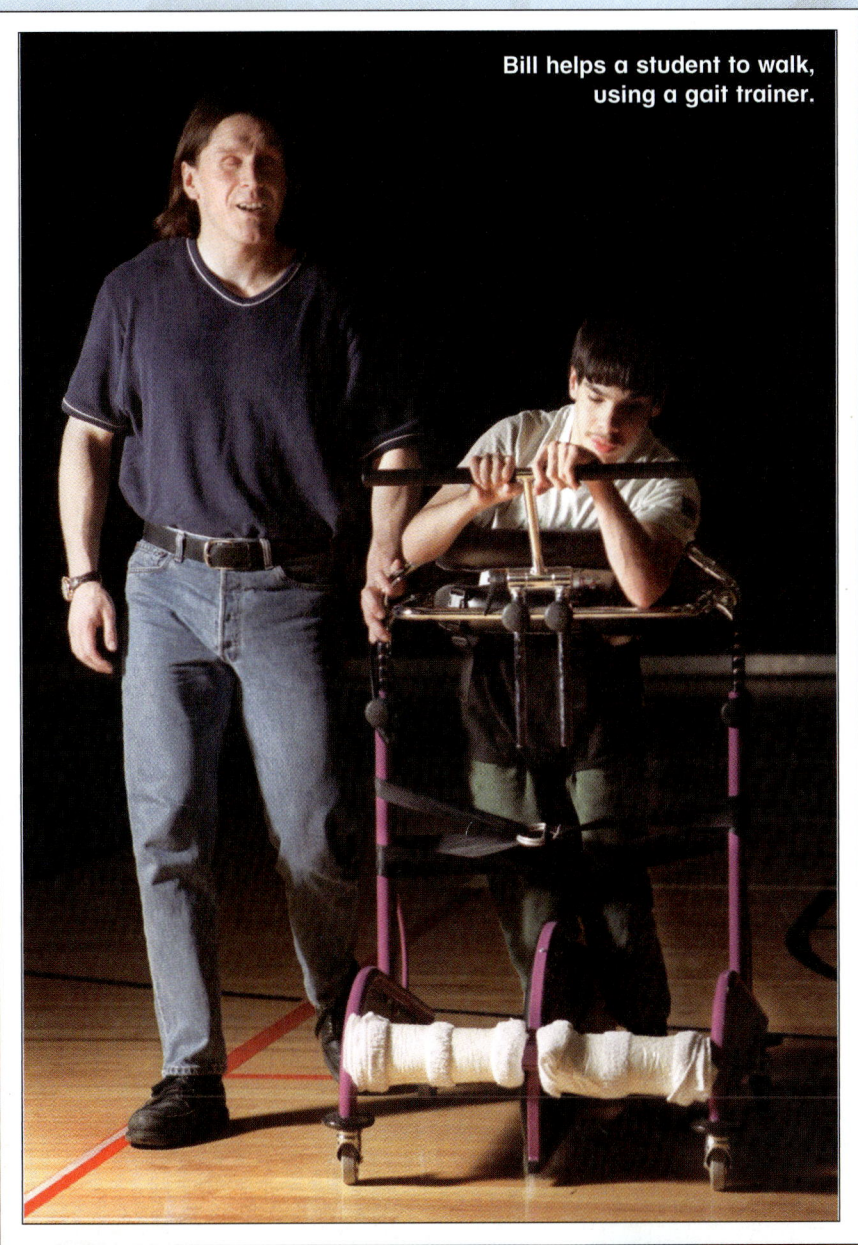

Bill helps a student to walk, using a gait trainer.

Laura: *Thanks very much for telling us about your school, Bill. Do you have anything else you'd like to tell us about sound?*

Bill: Here's something neat. If someone drops a coin on a table, I can tell from the sound what coin it is—quarter, nickel, dime—and even if it's Canadian or American. I know one of my students can do this, too, but I don't know if other people can.

Reflect on

Strategies: How did thinking about question-and-answer text pattern help you to understand the information in this interview?

Your Learning: How can you use what you learned in this article to be more aware of the sound messages around you?

119

Understanding media

Sounding Off

Identifying Point of View in Web Articles

Everyone has a personal point of view. Your point of view is the way you look at the world around you. You and your friends may have the same point of view about what makes a great movie. You and your parents may have different points of view about certain TV shows.

On these two pages, you'll read web articles about an invention called the Mosquito. As you read, notice the different points of view.

> Think about what ideas are missing. What does this text *not* say about teenagers?

eNews

Fed Up with Noisy Teenagers Hanging Around Your Store?

The Mosquito is the invention of Howard Stapleton. It gives off a high-frequency sound that sounds like a buzzing insect. Apparently, only people under 20 can hear the sound. The device is the perfect solution to the problem of young troublemakers. These noisy teens hang around outside stores and drive away paying customers.

> Look at the writer's word choice to help you figure out point of view. How are teenagers described in this web article?

Add your comment

Why spend hundreds of dollars on the Mosquito? I thought the easy (and cheap) way to keep teens from hanging around was to play classical or opera music on your store's sound system.

True Blue, Oak Ridges, ON

> Make inferences to discover point of view. What does this writer think about teenagers' tastes in music?

120 Sound

Read this web article about how some students used the Mosquito sound in an unexpected way. Look at the writer's word choice and make inferences to help you figure out the different points of view.

Sounds GOOD!

School children have hijacked a high–pitched alarm that cannot be heard by adults. They have created ringtones using this sound so they can get away with using cell phones in class.

Techno-savvy students have adapted the Mosquito alarm, used to drive teenage gangs away from shopping centres.

The alarm works because its ultra-high sound can be heard only by youths but not by most people over 20.

School children recorded the sound, which they named Teen Buzz, and spread it from phone to phone via text messages. Now they can receive calls and texts during class, and teachers have no idea what's going on.

One high-school teacher said, "All the kids were laughing about something, but I didn't know what. They know phones must be turned off during school. They could all hear somebody's phone ringing, but I couldn't hear a thing. One of the other children told me all about it later. I couldn't be too upset because it shows resourcefulness."

Inventor Howard Stapleton said, "I think it is a giggle."

Understanding speaking strategies

Making Meaning Clear

Words often have more than one meaning. When you are speaking, you want to make sure that your listener is thinking about the same meaning that you are. Sometimes, you need to add details to make the meaning of your words clear.

How to make sure your listener understands what you mean:

- ✓ Use the correct word.
- ✓ Think about whether the word could mean something else.
- ✓ Make sure you add enough details to make the meaning clear to your listener.

Musical Sounds

by Julian Rowe and Molly Perham

A musical instrument produces a sound by making the air around it vibrate.

Types of Instruments

- The strings of stringed instruments make the air vibrate when they are plucked or played with a bow.
- Wind instruments work when you blow on the column of air inside them.
- Percussion instruments have a tight piece of skin or plastic, or a piece of metal or wood. These make the air vibrate when you bang, scrape, or shake them.

Putting It All Together

As you read this article, remember to use the strategies you've learned in this unit:

- Monitor comprehension.
- Recognize strong verbs.
- Identify characteristics of question-and-answer text pattern.

How do these instruments make the air vibrate to make a sound?

harmonica, mandolin, djembe drum, French horn, tambourine, viola

How do Stringed Instruments Work?

This guitar player plucks the strings with the fingers of her right hand to make music. When a string is plucked, its vibrations cause sound waves in the air. As these waves reach our ears, we hear a note.

By pressing strings with the fingers of her left hand, the player makes the notes high or low.

Make a Guitar

What you need
- two large rubber bands
- two pencils
- a book

Stretch the rubber bands around the book. These will be the "strings." Push the pencils under the rubber bands. Press down one of the strings with your finger to change the length of the string that you pluck.

Plucking the short part of the string makes a high note.

Plucking the long part of the string makes a low note.

The rubber bands work much like the strings of a guitar.

How do Wind Instruments Work?

The recorder player blows the air inside the pipe to make music. He moves his fingers on and off the holes to produce different notes. When a hole is open near the top of the recorder, some of the air in the pipe escapes. When there is less air, the column of air inside vibrates quickly and produces a high note.

The flute is another wind instrument.

Make a Bottle Organ

What you need
- six plastic bottles that are the same size and shape

Stand the bottles in a line and pour different amounts of water into each one. Blow across the tops of the bottles. Each one makes a different note.

Which one makes the highest note?

Which one makes the lowest note?

How do PERCUSSION INSTRUMENTS work?

A drum has a piece of thin material called a drumhead stretched across the top. When you bang the drumhead, it vibrates and makes sound waves in the air. Before he plays, this drummer will turn a screw to make the drumhead tighter.

A tight drumhead vibrates faster and produces a high note. When it is looser, it vibrates more slowly and produces a low note.

hand drum

bongos

Make a Drum

What you need
- a hollow container— such as a bowl, saucepan, ice-cream container, or wastebasket
- plastic wrap
- tape or a strong rubber band
- wooden spoon

Stretch the plastic wrap tightly over the container to make the drumhead. Tape down the edges firmly, or use the rubber band.

Use the spoon for a drumstick.

Reflect on

Strategies: What strategies helped you understand the article? Was there a place you got stuck? What strategy did you use to help you?

Your Learning: You've just read an article about musical sounds. How could you use PowerPoint to present the information in a different way?

Sound

Credits

Text

p. 13: Reprinted with permission of the publisher, Children's Book Press, San Francisco, CA. *China's Bravest Girl* text © 1993 by Charlie Chin, illustrations © 1993 by Tomie Arai; p. 25: Text copyright © 1986 by Anne Rockwell. Used by permission of HarperCollins Publishers; p. 35: Reprinted with permission of the publisher, Children's Book Press, San Francisco, CA. *The Woman Who Outshone the Sun* by Alejandro Cruz Martinez. Illustrations copyright © 1991 by Fernando Olivera; p. 44: From Volume 4: WORLD BOOK'S YOUNG SCIENTIST © 2004 World Book, Inc. By permission of the publisher. www.worldbook.com; p. 46: Taken from *Science Experiments with Light*, published by Franklin Watts, a division of The Watts Publishing Group Ltd., 338 Euston Rd., London NW1 3BH; p. 64: From *Attack of the Killer Video Book*, published by Annick Press. Used by permission of Annick Press; p. 78: Material from *See Saw Saskatchewan* written by Robert Heidbreder is used by permission of Kids Can Press Ltd., Toronto. Text © 2003 Robert Heidbreder; p. 80: From *Fox on the Ice* published by HarperCollins Publishers Ltd. Text copyright © 2003 by Tomson Highway. Illustrations copyright © 2003 by Brian Deines. All rights reserved. Reprinted by permission of HarperCollins Publishers Ltd.; p. 84: Adapted from *Wow Canada!* by Vivien Bowers © 1999 with permission of the publisher Maple Tree Press Inc., Toronto, Canada; p. 96: From *By Truck to the North* by Andy Turnbull, published by Annick Press. Used by permission of Annick Press; p. 104: © The Child's World, www.childsworld.com; p. 107: Taken from *Sound and Music* by Barbara Taylor, published by Franklin Watts, a division of The Watts Publishing Group Ltd., 338 Euston Rd., London NW1 3BH; p. 110 From The Science of Sound, Weigl Publishers Ltd., Copyright 2000; p. 112: Copyright © 1996 by Shel Silverstein. Used by permission of HarperCollins Publishers. "Noise Day" by Shel Silverstein, from FALLING UP: Poems and Drawings by Shel Silverstein.Copyright © 1996 by Evil Eye Music, Inc.   By permission of Edite Kroll Literary Agency Inc.; p. 114: Material from *Sound Science* by Etta Kaner is used by permission of Kids Can Press Ltd., Toronto. Text © 1991 Etta Kaner; p. 123: Taken from *Making Sounds* by Julian Rowe and Molly Perham, published by Franklin Watts, a division of The Watts Publishing Group Ltd., 338 Euston Rd., London NW1 3BH

Photos

Cover: (tl) From China's Bravest Girl, Children's Book Press; (tr) © Royalty-Free/Corbis, (br) Ralph Wetmore/Stone/Getty Images, (bl) © Royalty-Free/Corbis; p. 7: Warner Bros/The Kobal Collection; p. 23: THE KOBAL COLLECTION / TOUCHSTONE PICTURES/JERRY BRUCKHEIMER FILMS; p. 24: PRNewsFoto/Square Enix, Inc.; p. 41: Ralph Wetmore/Stone/Getty Images; p. 44: Ralph H. Wetmore II/Stone/Getty Images; p. 45: Shutterstock; p. 46: (tray) Shutterstock, (tissue paper) Shutterstock, (bag) Shutterstock, (book) Shutterstock, (wood) Keith Goldstein/Getty Images, (girl) Kareem Black/Image Bank/Getty Images p. 48: (t) Shutterstock, (m) Photodisc/Getty Images,

(b) © Bettmann/CORBIS; p. 50: Courtesy of The Royal Astronomical Society of Canada; p. 51: © Roger Ressmeyer/CORBIS; p. 52: Shutterstock; p. 53: (t) Photos.com, (bl) Photos.com, (br) Photos.com; p. 54 (t) Estelle Rancurel/Taxi/Getty Images, (b) Paul Chesley/Stone/Getty Images; p. 55: (l) © Royalty-Free/Corbis; p. 56: (t) Shutterstock, (b) © Daniel Barillot/Masterfile; p. 59: (t) David Parker/Science Photo Library; (b) Photos.com; p. 62: © Jeff Daly/Visuals Unlimited; p. 63: © Royalty-free/Masterfile; p. 67: © Royalty-free/Corbis; p. 68: (flag) © Royalty-Free/Corbis, (license plate) © Carl & Ann Purcell/CORBIS, (oil derrick) © J. A. Kraulis/Masterfile, (cowboy) © Darrell Lecorre/Masterfile, (Stanley Cup) © Bettmann/CORBIS, (Confederation Bridge) © J. A. Kraulis/Masterfile, (portaging) Corel, (lobster) © Daryl Benson/Masterfile; p. 69: (lacrosse) Lawrence Migdale/Photoresearchers/First Light , (dreamcatcher) Shutterstock, (Perce Rock) Shutterstock, (sign) © Wolfgang Kaehler/CORBIS, (totem pole) Shutterstock, (wheat) Photos.com, (beaver) Photos.com, (L'anse aux Meadows) © Greg Probst/CORBIS, (whales) © Joel W. Rogers/CORBIS, (Lions Gate Bridge) © Albert Normandin/Masterfile, (Parliament) Shutterstock; p. 72: © J. David Andrews/Masterfile; pp. 72-73: © Garry Black/Masterfile; p. 73: © Peter Christopher/Masterfile; p. 75: © William Manning/CORBIS; p. 76: (background) © Sherman Hines/Masterfile, (t) © J. A. Kraulis/Masterfile, (b) © Brian Summers/First Light; p. 89: (t) Shutterstock, (m) Photos.com, (b) Brian Milne/First Light; p. 94: (t) Used by permission of Flight of Fancy, Nova Scotia, (b) © J. A. Kraulis/Masterfile; p. 95: (t) © Daryl Benson/Masterfile, (b) © Mark Hamblin/ A.G.E. Foto Stock/First Light, (leaf) © Robert Postma/First Light; pp. 96–100: All photos from *By Truck to the North* by Andy Turnbull, published by Annick Press, except p. 97: Photos.com, p. 98 (t) © Hans Blohm/Masterfile, p. 100: (c) Larry Macdougal/First Light; p. 101: © Bob Daemmrich/Photo Edit Inc.; p. 104 (t) Photos.com, (b) Photos.com; p. 105: Shutterstock; p. 106: Photos.com; p. 107: © Mark Tomalty/Masterfile; p. 108: © Joe McDonald/CORBIS; p. 110: Clipart.com; p. 111: Clipart.com, excerpt (cat) © Peter Lavery/Masterfile, (rattlesnake), (boy) Peter Ciresa/Index Stock; © Joe McDonald/CORBIS; p. 114: (t) © Royalty-Free/Corbis, (b) © NASA/Roger Ressmeyer/CORBIS; p. 115: (t) Shutterstock, (m) © Theo Allofs/Corbis, (b) © Underwood & Underwood/CORBIS; p. 116: (t) Photos.com, (b) Oliver Benn/Getty Images; p. 117: (t) CP Photo/COA/Jean Baptiste, (b) Steven Evans; p. 118: Steven Evans; p. 119: (t) Steven Evans, (b) Hamilton Spectator; p. 120: Courtesy of Compound Security Systems Ltd.; p.121: © Rolf Bruderer/Masterfile; p. 123: (all photos) Shutterstock; p. 124: (t) Photos.com, (b) Paul Simcock/Getty Images; p. 125: (t) Carlos Davila/Alamy, (b) Shutterstock; p. 126: (tl) Photos.com, (tr) Photos.com, (r) Andreas Kuehn/Taxi/Getty Images

Art

pp. 8–9: written and illustrated by Brian McLachlan; p. 19: illustrated by Brian McLachlan; p. 34: illustrated by Steve Manale; pp. 42–43: illustrated by Michael Cho; p. 49: illustrated by Steve Manale; pp. 50–51: illustrated by Jason Bone; p. 77: illustrated by Jason Bone; pp. 102–103: illustrated by Steve Manale; p. 109: illustrated by Jason Bone; p. 122: illustrated by Steve Manale